COOKING WITH CHILE PEPPERS

Coleen and Bob Simmons

BRISTOL PUBLISHING ENTERPRISES
San Leandro, California

a nitty gritty® cookbook

Printed in the United States of America.

ISBN 1-55867-149-8

Cover design: Frank J. Paredes
Cover photography: John A. Benson

CONTENTS

ALL ABOUT CHILES

When Columbus sailed the ocean blue in 1492, he was in search of spices, especially black pepper. Instead, he found members of the *Capsicum genus*. Although totally unrelated to black pepper, the new chiles, as the capsicum fruit came to be called, were immediately transported around the world by Spanish and Portuguese sailors, as well as over established land spice trade routes. The chile proved to be adaptable and hardy, and thrived in warm humid climates.

Chiles were soon integrated into the cuisines of North Africa, the Middle East, India and many tropical areas throughout the Pacific. Chiles promote thirst, encouraging liquid consumption, increase appetite and induce perspiration, helping to cool the body in hot climates. Chiles are considered a major source of vitamin C. Capsaicin, the heat source of the chile, is now marketed in skin creams for pain relief and soothing sore muscles. Other beneficial health effects such as lowering blood pressure and cholesterol, protection against blood clots, etc., have been attributed to the chile. After eating food spiced with hot chiles, some people experience a feeling of well-being, which is attributed to an "endorphin rush."

In Mexico, the Southwestern United States, the Caribbean, parts of Africa, India, Thailand and China, the hot chile pepper is a major star. Other areas of the world consume a milder chile pepper as an occasional condiment. Chiles generally add interest to starch-based cuisine. Rice and wheat are very bland foods and readily serve as a foil for spice, either added directly to a dish, or as a flavorful condiment. Many New World foods, particularly corn, tomatoes, potatoes, beans and avocados, go well with the flavor and spiciness of chiles. Old World onions, garlic and some spices and herbs — cumin, cilantro, and to a lesser extent, oregano — complement chiles. Hot chiles also accent the vegetable "pepper" taste of bell peppers when they are combined. These combinations occur frequently in our recipes.

Chile peppers today are enjoying tremendous popularity. New, fiery hot sauces are vying for market shelf space and each claims to be the best, the hottest, the ultimate taste experience. It would be impossible to categorize the huge array of hot sauces available, let alone give you any advice on what to buy for your taste. We have a few favorites that we keep on hand, which were selected as much for chile flavor as heat. These are included in our chile pantry list beginning on page 9. We suggest that you explore the available hot sauces, and buy and taste for yourself.

HOW HOT IS THE CHILE?

With the possible exception of major hot sauce products and Hungarian paprika, the spiciness of a product or a fresh chile is unpredictable. Fresh chiles, even those that look identical and are grown on the same plant, can vary drastically in heat. Climate, soil, growing season and cultivation all affect heat. Several varieties, particularly the jalapeño and habanero, have been hybridized to yield milder fruit. There is no way to tell by looking how hot a chile is, and each taster has a different heat threshold. For our taste, the jalapeño is medium-hot and 1 chile generally yields 1 tbs., finely chopped, which is enough to nicely spice many dishes. The serrano is hotter, and we would use 2 jalapeños instead of 1 serrano in most dishes. We usually discard the stem and scoop out the seeds, which tend to be bitter and devoid of chile flavor. The tiny Thai chile is extremely hot and the habanero is dynamite, so use them with care.

To find out how hot your particular chile is, cut off a very small piece and touch it to your tongue. If you get a strong stinging sensation, you may wish to cut back on the amount called for in the recipe. If there is just a little bite on your tongue, adjust the amount of chile upward. Generally, the smaller and thinner-skinned the chile, the hotter it is. Chiles become one to two times more intense in heat as they mature and turn from green to orange or red. Chiles with pointed ends tend to be hotter than those with blunt tips.

Chiles can be rated in Scoville Units, but there can be a wide variation, depending on the testing method used. Generally, dried ancho and New Mexico chiles are rated at 1,000 Scoville units; poblano at 2,500 units, chipotle at 10,000 and chile de arbol at 25,000 units. A fresh jalapeño is between 2,500 and 5,000 and the habanero can be rated as high as 300,000 units.

To put out a spicy chile fire in your mouth, milk or yogurt is much better than water, beer or wine. You can also eat a piece of bread, a cracker or some rice.

HANDLING HOT CHILES

While improper handling of chiles rarely causes long-term injury, it can result in very painful temporary consequences. Caution is the key word. If you are not certain how hot a chile is, treat it as potentially dangerous.

When cutting or handling hot chiles, wear thin rubber or plastic gloves. Special caution should be exercised by contact lens wearers. Take out your lenses before preparing extra hot chiles. Removing contacts, even several hours later, can be a painful experience. After handling hot chiles, always wash your hands with soap and plenty of hot water. To test for chile residue, touch your washed fingertips to your tongue. If it doesn't burn, you are okay. If you are working with a small amount of chile, slip a sandwich baggie over your hands, or use a knife and fork.

BUYING AND STORAGE OF FRESH CHILES

Always buy the freshest chiles available. The skins should be firm and shiny, not soft or withered-looking. There should be no signs of mold or soft spots. One of the best ways to keep fresh chiles is to store them, unwashed, in a perforated vegetable storage bag in the refrigerator vegetable drawer. Depending on how fresh they were at time of purchase, chiles usually keep for at least a week. Placing them in a paper bag before refrigerating is another suggested method. Immediately discard any moldy or soft chiles as they will hasten the spoilage of the other chiles in the same bag.

Of the two hundred or so different chiles in the world, a limited number of fresh or dried chiles are found in North American markets. To add to the chile confusion, the same chiles are called different names in different areas, making it easier to identify a chile by physical description rather than a specific name. As the interest in chiles and chile products grows, we expect that there will be new chile varieties coming to market. We have listed the fresh and dried chiles that seem to be widely available.

FRESH CHILES

Jalapeño: [ha la PEN yo] This is the best known and most widely available chile in our markets. It is typically about 2 to 3 inches long and 1 to 1½ inches wide, with a blunt end. It has a dark green color that turns to red when it matures. It is used fresh, roasted or pickled (escabèche). It is found whole or diced in cans. This is the chile used for nacho slices and rings. Heat intensity ranges from medium-hot to hot. Chipotle chiles are fresh ripe jalapeños that have been dried and smoked. Substitute serrano or Fresno chiles if you don't have a jalapeño.

Serrano: Bright green or red in color, this chile is a thin cylinder about 2 inches long and ½-inch wide. It is considered hot to very hot. It is used fresh in sauces, salsas and guacamole. Substitute 1 or 2 jalapeños or 1 Fresno chile in its place.

Anaheim: This is also called a California chile. It is bright green in color, or can be red, about 7 or 8 inches long and 2 inches wide. It is mild to medium-hot. Roast and peel, use in sauces or stuff to make *chiles rellenos*. This is the chile used in canned green chiles. Substitute a poblano chile if you are looking for a hotter chile to stuff.

Poblano: This chile's deep green color changes to red or brown as it matures. With wide shoulders, almost heart-shaped, the poblano is about 4 inches long and 2½ inches wide and the tip tapers to a blunt point. It varies from mild to hot, and should be roasted and peeled before eating. If it is very hot, remove veins and seeds before eating. It is stuffed, used for chile strips or added to soups and sauces. An Anaheim chile is a good substitute, but it is usually milder. *Poblanos are often mislabeled pasillas in markets.*

Fresno: Yellow-green to red in color, the Fresno is sometimes mistaken for a red jalapeño. It is about 2 to 3 inches long and 1½ inches wide at the shoulders, with a pointed tip. It has thick flesh and is considered hot. It is used fresh in salsas and sauces, or pickled. Jalapeños and serranos would be good substitutes.

Cayenne: This is a long, curved, dark green or red chile, about 5 or 6 inches long and

½-inch wide. The thin flesh is sometimes wrinkled. This chile ranges from hot to very hot and is related to the Tabasco chile, from which Tabasco Sauce is made. Substitute Thai or serrano chiles. It is used in salsas, and dried and ground to make cayenne pepper. It flavors Creole, Cajun, Szechwan, Hunan, Indian and Thai dishes.

Habanero: As this small lantern-shaped chile ripens, the color ranges from green to yellow-orange, orange or red. It is about 1 to 2 inches long and 1 to 2 inches wide, with a tiny pointed tip on its blunt end. It is a close relative to the Jamaican Scotch bonnet. Habaneros are very aromatic and are thought to be the hottest fresh pepper in North America. Use with care and do not handle with bare hands. Their primary use is in jerk seasoning and table sauces, and sometimes in very small quantities in salsa.

Thai: Thin, cylindrical, medium green to orange and red in color, this very hot small chile packs a wallop. It is about 1 to 2 inches long, and ¼-inch wide, with a long stem and pointed tip. It is used fresh, without removing seeds, to flavor stews, curries and dipping sauces and is an essential ingredient in Thai dishes.

DRIED CHILES

Ancho: This is the dried poblano, a mild to medium-hot chile. It has a rich, sweet, almost fruity flavor and is used with other chiles to help round out a sauce. It is one of the three chiles always used for mole sauces. It is also used for enchilada sauces and ground for commercial chili powders. A mulato chile is a suggested substitute.

Chile de arbol: This small, bright red chile is used dried. It is about 2 to 4 inches long and ¾-inch wide, with a long stem and pointed tip. It is very hot and is used to flavor vinegars and hot sauces.

Chipotle: [chi POTE lay] Ripe jalapeños are dried by slow smoking in ovens or over dried chile plant fires to obtain a smoky, rich, almost meaty, flavor. Chipotles are often found canned in adobo, a sauce made of vinegar, tomato, onions and spices. Dried chipotles are more difficult to rehydrate than other dried chiles. Cover dried chipotles with very hot water and soak for at least 1 hour.

Cascabel: Fresh, this chile resembles a red cherry, and it dries to a dark reddish brown. Its name means "jingle bell" because the seeds shake around inside. It is about 1 inch in diameter. It has a medium-hot, nutty flavor and is ground for sauces.

Guajillo: [gwa HEE yo] This hot dried chile is about 5 inches long and 1 inch wide, with smooth reddish-brown skin. It is used partly because of its rich red color and only a small amount is needed to flavor chili con carne, soups, stews and sauces.

Mulato: This looks similar to both the ancho and pasilla and ranges from mild to hot.

It is about 4 inches long and 2½ inches wide, darker brown than the ancho, and has a slightly sharp bite. It is one of the major components of a mole.

New Mexico: This chile is also called Californian or Colorado. It is about 5 to 6 inches long and 1 inch wide, with bright to dark brick red, slightly wrinkled skin. Medium hot, its flavor ranges from tomatoes to berries. It adds considerable flavor to sauces, and is ground as chile powder or crushed into red pepper flakes. New Mexico chiles are tied into bunches to make *ristras.*

Pasilla: This chile is also called *chile negro* because it is almost black. It is about 6 to 8 inches long and 1 to 2 inches wide. Used in moles, it gives the sauce its dark chocolate color. It is also used in other cooked sauces and soups.

THE CHILE PANTRY

Tabasco Classic Sauce: This has been a standard around the world for over a hundred years. It is quite hot, but doesn't have a lot of chile flavor. A drop or two is useful to adjust the heat in recipes containing fresh or dried chiles.

Tabasco Jalapeño Sauce: Introduced a few years ago, this light green sauce has become one of our favorites. It is not nearly as hot as the classic Tabasco, but with much more chile flavor. It is especially good on eggs and in cheese dishes.

Hot chile oil: This is oil infused with hot dried chile flakes or whole hot red chiles. The commercial brands usually found in Asian markets have a brilliant deep orange color which is mostly food coloring. We have included a recipe for a homemade version that we think is a superior product. A few drops of hot chile oil can be added to other fat used for sautés. Brush it on tortilla chips or toasts, or use it to make popcorn.

Sriracha sauce: Found in Asian markets, this is a bright orange-colored sauce made of chiles, vinegar and garlic. It has a good acidic flavor and moderately hot chile taste. Use it as you would Tabasco.

Sambal oelek: This bright, fresh, ground chile paste of Indonesian origin has loads of flavor and makes a piquant addition to many spicy dishes. Found in Asian markets and many supermarkets, it is also considered an acceptable substitute for the fiery hot Moroccan *harissa*. Add it to stir-fry dishes, scrambled eggs and hamburgers.

Harissa: This is a fiery hot North African chile paste, based on dried red chiles. It is available in a convenient tube or small cans.

Chile paste with garlic: This Asian condiment is a fermented bean, red chile and garlic mixture. A small amount adds considerable punch and rounds out stir-fry dishes containing meat or eggplant.

Chipotle peppers in adobo sauce: Dried smoked jalapeño chiles are canned in a vinegar and tomato sauce. A spoonful or two livens marinades, sauces and dips. This keeps well in the refrigerator after opening.

Red pepper flakes: These flakes vary from medium to extremely hot, and usually made from the New Mexico chile, including the seeds. They can be added to a dish during cooking, or sprinkled over a finished dish. More flavor is released when flakes are simmered in the liquid or fat used in the dish. They lose potency with exposure to air. Find them on supermarket spice shelves, labeled "crushed red pepper."

Cider vinegar: This milder fruity vinegar adds the right note of sweetness to many chile dishes. Rice vinegar is another favorite.

CHILE POWDERS AND SPICES

Pure chile powder: Pure chile powder does not include cumin, garlic, salt and other flavorings found in the more commonly used *chili* powder. Pure chile powders are made from ground dried chile pods. There are myriad varieties available, ranging from mild to super-hot. All types of chiles can be used to make chile powder, from the milder ancho and pasilla through cayenne and the hottest habanero. There are also chile powders made from smoked dried chiles.

The recipes in this book have been tested with a chile powder labeled "New Mexican chile powder — medium hot." A dark brick red color, it adds complex, almost fruity overtones as well as heat to a dish. Pasilla chile powder is similar in heat and flavor.

To make your own pure chile powder, open the dried chile and shake out the seeds. Remove the stem, break the chile into pieces and grind it to powder with an electric coffee grinder or spice mill.

Cayenne pepper has been available in supermarkets for years. Like Tabasco Sauce, it does not seem to have a great deal of chile character. It is often used to add heat to a dish that contains other more flavorful chiles.

Cumin is a chile pantry essential. It is originally from the Middle East, and is very aromatic. Cumin is a flavor component of most prepared chili powders because it blends so well with chile flavors. It is also found in curry powder mixtures. It is worth the effort to toast and crush whole cumin seeds just before adding to a dish.

Dried Mexican oregano is a pungent herb used in salsas and other Southwestern and Mexican dishes. It is stronger than the Mediterranean or Greek oregano, and goes particularly well with tomatoes, corn and chiles. Crush it with your fingers to release its full flavor before adding it to a dish.

CHILE SOURCES

- Local farmers' markets are a great source for home-grown chiles, particularly during late summer, when chiles are in season.
- Ethnic markets, particularly Asian, Indian, Caribbean and Middle Eastern carry fresh and dried products for their cuisines.
- Internet: Search for chile peppers, also for providers of plants and seeds.
- Major seed companies are good sources for gardeners: Burpee, Gurney, Park and Stokes.

Fire Alley
13207 Ventura Blvd.
Studio City, CA 91604
818-986-HEAT
E-mail: fiery@firealley.com

Hot sauces, salsas and everything about using chile peppers; brochure and order form available

Chile Today Hot Tamale
919 Highway 33, Suite 47
Freehold, NJ 07728
800-HOT-PEPPER
800-468-7377

Chile peppers, chile powders, gift boxes, sampler packs; brochure and order form available

Frieda's by Mail
800-241-1771
E-mail: friedas@aol.com

Fresh and dried chiles, catalog available

Redwood City Seed Company
P. O. Box 361
Redwood City, CA 94064
415-325-7333
http://www.batnet.com/rwc-seed

Chile seeds and powdered chiles;
catalog available

Chile Pepper Magazine
P. O. Box 769
Mt. Morris, IL 61054-0769
800-959-5468

A good informative magazine dedi-
cated to chiles. Interesting articles,
recipes and many ads for up-to-date
mail order spices, sauces and chiles

WHAT TO DRINK WITH SPICY CHILE DISHES

Beer is the first thing that comes to mind when choosing a beverage to accompany spicy dishes. The flavors are harmonious and the bubbles help to clean and refresh the palate. Light wheat-based beers, sold as weisbeers or witbeer, are particularly good with medium-hot chile dishes.

Crisp, slightly sweet wines such as white Riesling or Gewurztraminer go well with mildly spicy fish or chicken dishes. Sauvignon Blanc accents herb and vegetable components in a dish and will stand up to robust flavors. Champagne or sparkling wine pairs extremely well with spicy appetizers, and fish or poultry dishes.

Slightly chilled light, fruity white Zinfandel and rose wines complement spicy barbecue dishes. Aged, expensive red wines will be overpowered by the chile heat. Save them for simpler roasts or sauced dishes.

Another interesting beverage combination is a mixture of equal parts tomato juice and beer. The tomato juice helps to moderate and complement the chile heat. Indian cuisines are often accompanied by chilled yogurt- or buttermilk-based drinks, called *lassi*, flavored with fruit or herbs.

SCOPE OF THIS BOOK

We grew up in the Midwest and weren't introduced to anything more spicy than black pepper, which was used sparingly. It was a revelation when we moved to San Francisco in the 1950s and discovered taco sauce and a whole array of Mexican food items in the supermarket. The interest in chiles and chile-based products has exploded in the last 15 years. While we aren't real "chile heads," we do love well-seasoned foods. We have drawn inspiration from many cuisines for these recipes, but do not claim to have included "authentic" recipes. This is the way we like to cook in California.

BASIC PREPARATION TECHNIQUES

This is quick reference guide to several basic techniques used throughout *Cooking With Chile Peppers*. These preparations can be done a day or two ahead and refrigerated. It is a great time-saver to roast corn, garlic or tomatoes when you are using the oven for other dishes. When tomatoes and peppers are in season, buy extra and roast and freeze some for later. If you are using vegetables for a pasta sauce or casserole, freezing won't affect the finished product, and there will be more flavor because the produce was harvested at peak of season. Frozen roasted red or yellow bell peppers are a delight to have on hand for pizza, salads, sandwiches or a garnish. Chipotle puree keeps for 2 or 3 weeks in the refrigerator, and if you have it, a spoonful will give a smoky flavor to sauces, vegetable or meat dishes. Chipotles have a great affinity for beans, eggplant and tomatoes. Dried chiles, too, have intense flavor when reconstituted, and can be pureed for winter sauces, soups or salsas.

PREPARING ROASTED PEPPERS AND CHILES
Red, yellow and green bell peppers, green Anaheim chiles and poblano chiles all roast or char beautifully. Jalapeño chiles can be roasted, but the skin is not tough, making peeling unnecessary. Peppers and chiles can be roasted on a medium-hot grill, under the broiler, or suspended on a fork over a stovetop gas flame. Grilling and

broiling are easier and make fewer drips on the stove.

To grill: Preheat grill or prepare a barbecue fire. Roast peppers and chiles on grill rack, turning with tongs so the skin is nicely charred on all sides. If fire is extremely hot, raise grill rack and turn more frequently. The goal is to char the skin quickly without burning the flesh.

To broil: Preheat broiler. Line a shallow baking pan or cookie sheet with foil, and place peppers and chiles on a rack. Broil about 6 inches from source of heat. Turn until skin is nicely charred on all sides.

To peel: Remove charred peppers and chiles from heat, place in a large bowl, cover bowl with foil and steam peppers and chiles for 10 to 15 minutes or longer for easier peeling. Pull off outer skin and discard stems and seeds. The chile pepper juices have a lot of flavor, so drain them into a storage container with the chiles. In order to preserve the nice smoky flavor, don't rinse the peppers or chiles under running water.

To store: Place peeled peppers and chiles in a covered storage container and refrigerate for 4 to 5 days, or freeze.

PREPARING ROASTED AND OVEN-DRIED TOMATOES

To roast: Both plum (roma) and regular tomatoes can be roasted. Leave tomatoes whole. Because it is desirable to catch the tomato juices and use them for sauce or salsas, it is easier to broil the tomatoes rather than grilling them. Preheat broiler. Line a rimmed shallow baking pan with foil and place tomatoes on foil. Broil about 6 inches from heat source until tomatoes are blackened on all sides. They will collapse and turn a very dark color. Remove from broiler and cool slightly. Roasted tomatoes and juice can be stored in a covered container for 2 or 3 days in the refrigerator until ready to be used.

If making puree, remove tomato cores and pour tomatoes with skins and juice into a blender or food processor container. Process until smooth or as directed in recipe.

To oven-dry: Oven-dried tomatoes have an intense, bright flavor, and we prefer them to purchased sun-dried tomatoes. Plum (roma) and small regular tomatoes work best for oven-drying. Preheat oven to 275°. Line a rimmed shallow baking pan with foil. Core tomatoes, cut plum tomatoes in half and larger tomatoes in quarters and remove most of the seeds with your fingers. Place cut-side up in baking pan. Sprinkle with your choice of topping: salt and pepper, *Chili Salt*, page 130, a little olive oil and finely minced garlic, or olive oil and herbs. Bake for 2½ to 3 hours, until tomatoes feel leathery, but are still soft and pliable. Remove from oven and cool. Store in an airtight container in the refrigerator for 3 to 4 days, or freeze. Use in place of sun-dried tomatoes in recipes. Sliver and scatter over pizza, or add to pastas, salads or salsas.

PREPARING ROASTED ONIONS

Onions can be oven-roasted to a delectable sweet soft consistency. Preheat oven to 275°. Do not peel, but cut onions in half. Brush cut sides with a little olive oil and place cut side down on foil in a rimmed shallow baking pan. Bake for 1 to 1½ hours, until onions are soft to the touch. These can be done at the same time you are oven-drying tomatoes. Remove skin from roasted onions and use thin slices on pizza and in pasta, or puree and add to sauces and salsas. Refrigerate for 3 to 4 days.

PREPARING ROASTED GARLIC

Roast 2 or 3 whole heads of garlic while you are using the oven for another purpose. Tightly covered, roasted garlic keeps well in the refrigerator for 1 week. Remove a few of the papery outside leaves of the garlic head, but do not peel. With a sharp knife cut off about ½ inch from top, exposing tops of cloves. Drizzle full-flavored olive oil over cut surface, wrap each head tightly in foil and bake at 275° to 400° for 30 to 45 minutes, or until garlic feels soft when squeezed through the foil. Allow to cool. Squeeze pulp out of cloves as needed. Roasted garlic is a natural for mashed potatoes, pasta sauces, bruschetta, salad dressings and marinades.

PREPARING CHIPOTLE PUREE

Chipotle chiles in adobo sauce provide chile spice and a wonderful smoky flavor to many dishes. To make them easier to measure, puree the chipotles with the sauce. Using rubber or plastic gloves, remove stems, cut chiles in half and discard most of the seeds. Place cleaned chiles and adobo sauce in a food processor or blender container and process until smooth. Pour into a clean jar, cover and refrigerate for 1 to 2 weeks.

PREPARING OVEN-ROASTED CORN

When fresh sweet corn is in season, try roasting it for salads, salsas, pizzas and quesadillas. We like to use the tender white corn, but yellow is delicious also. This makes about 1 cup and can be done 3 to 4 days in advance, and refrigerated until needed. Preheat oven to 425°. Line a rimmed shallow baking pan with foil. Cut kernels from 3 or 4 ears of corn into baking pan and add 2 tbs. olive oil, salt and pepper. Toss corn, coating well with oil, and spread it out in an even layer. Bake for 15 to 18 minutes, stirring once or twice, until corn is lightly browned. Remove from oven and cool slightly.

Petite frozen corn can also be roasted. It has a nice flavor, but the texture may be slightly more firm than fresh corn. Thaw before roasting.

RECONSTITUTING DRIED CHILES

Dried chiles are easily softened and plumped. Check packages of stored dried chiles frequently to make sure there aren't tiny webs or other evidence of bugs. If you find some, discard the whole package. Remove dried chiles from package, lightly rinse under running water to remove any dust and pat dry. Remove stems, slit chiles, if necessary, and shake out seeds. Heat a heavy skillet over medium heat and lightly toast each side of the chile for 20 or 30 seconds until it softens. Do not allow chiles to burn or they will have a bitter taste. Tear each chile into 2 or 3 pieces and place in a small bowl. Cover with boiling water and soak for 20 to 30 minutes. Make sure chiles are submerged in water. Carefully remove chiles from soaking liquid, leaving sand and dirt in the bottom of bowl. Discard soaking liquid unless called for in the recipe.

COOKING POULTRY DISHES WITH CHILES

Chicken in its many forms, whether roasted, baked or grilled, pairs beautifully with fresh or dried chiles. One technique involves stuffing a spicy mixture under the skin of a whole roasting chicken or chicken pieces so it bastes the meat during cooking. *Roast Chicken With Chile Goat Cheese Stuffing* results in a moist, nicely spiced bird.

Chicken thighs are marinated and baked in a hot oven rather than grilled, because of the time required to thoroughly cook chicken to a safe internal temperature. *Moroccan-Style Roasted Chicken* has a yogurt-based marinade, and *New Mexico Chile Chicken* is coated with a dried chile mixture.

For a change of pace, try *Spicy Chicken Curry* and serve it with the traditional curry accompaniments of basmati rice, chutney, chopped nuts, marinated raisins and a fruit salad. *Thai Chicken Wrap* has a spicy chicken filling tucked into a large flour tortilla that can be eaten warm or at room temperature. *Santa Fe Pizza* makes good use of leftover chicken.

Cornish game hens are smaller and grill more quickly than regular chickens. They are particularly succulent when grilled over charcoal with a Middle Eastern-flavored marinade.

MOROCCAN-STYLE ROASTED CHICKEN

Servings: 4

Chicken thighs are marinated in a fragrant yogurt-based marinade and baked in a very hot oven, tandoori-style. Harissa, a fiery hot North African chile paste, is available in a convenient tube or small cans.

MARINADE

2 cloves garlic
1/2 tsp. salt
1 cup plain yogurt
grated peel (zest) and juice of 1 orange
1 tbs. sherry vinegar

1 tbs. peeled, finely chopped ginger root
1 tsp. ground coriander
1 tsp. ground cumin
1/4 tsp. turmeric
1/2 tsp. harissa

8 chicken thighs, skin removed, trimmed of fat

Mince garlic with salt to form a paste. Combine garlic with remaining marinade ingredients and mix well. Place chicken in a locking plastic bag and pour in marinade, turning to coat pieces evenly. Refrigerate for 6 to 8 hours or overnight. Remove from refrigerator 30 minutes before cooking. Preheat oven to 500°. Line a rimmed baking sheet with foil. Place a rack over foil and spray with nonstick cooking spray. Remove chicken from marinade, place on rack and roast for 15 minutes. Turn chicken pieces over and continue to roast for 20 minutes until juices are clear when thighs are pierced.

NEW MEXICO CHILE CHICKEN

*Flavors of the Southwest are used in this marinade. Serve with **Chiles and Rice**, page 99, or **Black Bean and Roasted Corn Salad**, page 94, and a crisp green salad. Cilantro stems have a lot of flavor, and are included here.*

MARINADE

2 dried New Mexico chiles, reconstituted (see instructions page 20)
1/4 cup rice vinegar
2 tbs. vegetable oil
2 tsp. honey

1 cup coarsely chopped cilantro leaves and stems, loosely packed
salt and freshly ground pepper
1 tsp. dried oregano
water as needed, optional

8 chicken thighs, skin removed, fat trimmed

Place drained chiles in a blender container with marinade ingredients. Process until well combined. If mixture is too thick to pour, add 1 to 2 tbs. water. Pour over chicken and mix well. Cover and refrigerate for 2 to 3 hours. Remove from refrigerator 30 minutes before cooking. Preheat oven to 400°. Line a rimmed baking sheet with foil and place a rack over foil; spray with nonstick cooking spray. Arrange chicken on rack and roast, turning once, for 40 to 45 minutes or until internal temperature reaches 185° and juices are clear when thighs are pierced.

SPICY CHICKEN CURRY

*Serve with steamed basmati rice, **Mango and Red Pepper Chutney**, page 154, some chopped almonds and marinated raisins or dried cherries. If you like, remove the cooked chicken meat from the bone and return it to the sauce before serving.*

1/4 cup butter
2 medium onions, chopped
1 large carrot, peeled, finely chopped
1 stalk celery, finely chopped
1-2 tbs. finely chopped red Fresno or jalapeño chile
2 cloves garlic, finely chopped
2-3 tbs. curry powder
1 medium-sized tart apple, peeled, finely chopped
8 chicken thighs, skin removed
1 3/4 cups chicken broth
1 tbs. tomato paste
1 tbs. cornstarch dissolved in 1 tbs. cold water, optional
salt and pepper
slivered fresh basil leaves for garnish
2 cups basmati rice, cooked according to package directions
assorted condiments: fresh fruit salsa or chutney, toasted coconut, toasted
    chopped nuts, marinated raisins or other dried fruit, bacon bits, chopped egg

Melt butter in a large, heavy nonaluminum saucepan. Cook onions over medium heat for about 5 minutes to soften. Add carrot, celery and chiles. Cook for 5 minutes and add garlic and curry powder. Stir and cook just until curry releases its fragrance. Add apple, chicken thighs, chicken broth and tomato paste. Bring mixture to a boil, lower heat, cover and simmer for about 30 to 35 minutes until chicken is cooked. Serve thighs whole or debone, discard bones and cut each thigh into 6 pieces. If sauce seems thin, thicken by stirring in a little of the cornstarch mixture. Cook for an additional 2 to 3 minutes. Adjust seasoning with salt and pepper, pour into a heated serving bowl and top with slivered fresh basil leaves. Spoon over cooked rice. The condiments can be sprinkled over the curry, or placed by the spoonful on the side of the plate.

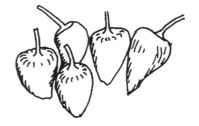

ROAST CHICKEN WITH
CHIPOTLE CILANTRO STUFFING

Servings: 3-4

A spicy smoked chile and cilantro paste stuffed under the skin bastes the chicken while it is roasting. Use thin rubber or plastic gloves to avoid irritation when stuffing chile paste under chicken skin. Serve with buttered new potatoes and creamed peas.

1 whole frying chicken, about 3½ lb.
1 tsp. olive oil
1 tbs. *Chipotle Puree*, page 19
grated peel (zest) from 1 orange
1 tbs. orange juice

¼ cup coarsely chopped cilantro leaves
  and stems
1 tsp. peeled, grated ginger root
1 clove garlic, minced
salt and freshly ground pepper

Preheat oven to 375°. Remove giblets and excess fat from chicken cavity. Wash chicken under cold running water and pat dry. Using fingertips, gently make a pocket between breast skin and meat, working all the way down over thighs. Combine remaining ingredients in a small bowl and mix well. Start at top of breast and stuff paste under skin. Gently massage paste down both sides of breast meat and over thighs to form an even layer. Place chicken breast-side up in a roasting pan on a rack and roast for about 1 hour, or until internal temperature reaches 185°. Allow chicken to rest for several minutes before carving.

ROAST CHICKEN WITH
CHILE GOAT CHEESE STUFFING

Servings: 4

Any roasted, peeled fresh chile can be used in this dish, or use mild, canned, diced green chiles.

1 whole frying chicken, about 3½ lb.
2 tbs. finely minced fresh red or green
    chiles
4 oz. fresh goat cheese
2-3 tsp. milk
1 green onion, white part only, minced

1 tbs. lime juice
¼ tsp. Tabasco Jalapeño Sauce
1 tbs. chopped fresh parsley
1 tbs. chopped cilantro
salt and freshly ground pepper

Preheat oven to 375°. Remove giblets and excess fat from chicken. Wash chicken under cold running water and pat dry. Using fingertips, gently loosen skin and make a pocket between breast skin and meat, working all the way down over thighs. Combine remaining ingredients in a small bowl and mix well. Starting at top of breast, stuff paste under skin. Gently massage filling down both sides of breast meat and over thighs to form an even layer. Place chicken breast side up in a roasting pan on a rack and roast for about 1 hour, or until internal temperature reaches 185°. Allow chicken to rest for several minutes before carving.

COOKING POULTRY DISHES WITH CHILES 29

THAI CHICKEN WRAP

A savory chicken and salad filling is folded into large tortillas for a satisfying lunch. These are picked up and eaten at room temperature. Use smaller tortillas to make great party fare for a group. Thai chiles are extremely hot and just one will flavor this dish. Use gloves or knife and fork to handle.

PEANUT SAUCE

1/3 cup chicken broth
1/3 cup creamy peanut butter
1 tbs. minced peeled ginger root
1 small clove garlic, minced
1 tbs. soy sauce
1 tbs. lime juice
1 tbs. rice vinegar
2 tsp. brown sugar
1 small Thai chile, or 2 serrano chiles, stemmed, with seeds, finely minced

Combine all ingredients with a blender or food processor. Process until smooth.

1-1½ cups shredded cooked chicken
3 cups finely shredded napa cabbage
⅓ cup coarsely grated cucumber, blotted with paper towels
2 tbs. coarsely chopped unsalted dry roasted peanuts
¼ cup coarsely chopped cilantro leaves
4 flour tortillas, 8-9 inch diameter

In a large bowl, toss chicken, cabbage, cucumber, peanuts and cilantro with *Peanut Sauce* until well mixed. Heat tortillas for 15 to 20 seconds each side in a dry hot skillet until softened. Spoon chicken filling on bottom third of each tortilla. Fold in sides, fold up bottom and roll up burrito-style. Serve whole, or diagonally cut each wrap in half horizontally to make 2 smaller, easier-to-eat pieces.

SANTA FE PIZZA

Leftover chicken or turkey pairs with Southwestern flavors for a quick pizza.

1 recipe pizza crust, page 44
2 cups coarsely grated mozzarella cheese
1/3 cup pine nuts
1 tbs. Tabasco Jalapeño Sauce
2 tsp. lime juice
1 tsp. olive oil
1/2 tsp. chile powder
2 cups thinly sliced cooked chicken
  (sliced across grain)

8-10 oven-roasted tomatoes, page 17,
  or sun-dried tomatoes, cut into slivers
1/3 cup thin strips roasted red peppers,
  page 17, or purchased
1 small red onion, peeled, very thinly
  sliced
salt and freshly ground pepper
1/3 cup grated Parmesan or aged (dry)
  Monterey Jack cheese

Preheat oven to 450° with pizza stone, if using. Make pizza dough and roll out into 2 circles, each about 11 inches in diameter. Place each round on a piece of foil. Distribute mozzarella cheese over each crust and sprinkle with pine nuts. Combine Tabasco, lime juice, olive oil and chili powder with chicken; toss to coat chicken pieces. Scatter chicken over crusts and add tomatoes, red peppers and onion slices. Season with salt and pepper and sprinkle with Parmesan cheese. Bake pizzas on a pizza stone or baking sheet for about 12 to 15 minutes, until pizza crust is nicely browned. If using a baking sheet, bake on the lowest oven shelf.

GRILLED CORNISH GAME HENS

Here is a quick, spicy, lemon-flavored marinade for game hens or small chickens.

2 Cornish game hens, about 1¼ lb. each

MARINADE
2 tbs. full-flavored olive oil
¼ cup lemon juice
1 clove garlic, finely chopped
1 tsp. sambal oelek (see page 10)

pinch cinnamon
½ tsp. ground coriander
½ tsp. ground cumin
salt and freshly ground pepper

With kitchen shears, remove backbone from game hens, open up and flatten breast bone with the palm of your hand. Wash hens, pat dry and place in a nonaluminum pan or locking plastic bag. Add marinade ingredients to a blender or food processor container and process until well blended. Pour marinade over hens, coating both sides. Cover and refrigerate for 2 to 3 hours, turning over once or twice. Remove from refrigerator about 30 minutes before grilling.

Cook game hens on a preheated grill over medium heat for about 15 to 20 minutes each side, or until meat is no longer pink and internal temperature reaches 180° on a meat thermometer.

TURKEY AND WHITE BEAN CHILI

Servings: 4-6

Here is a great way to use up some of the Thanksgiving turkey leftovers. This hearty soup cooks in less than 30 minutes and makes a very satisfying cold weather lunch or supper.

2 tbs. vegetable oil
1 cup diced onion
4 cloves garlic, minced
3-4 tbs. finely chopped jalapeño chiles
1 tbs. ground cumin
1 tsp. dried oregano
1½ cups frozen or fresh corn kernels
1 can (7 oz.) diced green chiles with juice
4 cups chicken broth
2 cans (15 oz. each) small white beans with juice
2 cups diced cooked turkey or chicken, in ½-inch cubes
1 tsp. Tabasco Jalapeño Sauce
salt and freshly ground pepper
fresh cilantro leaves for garnish
grated Monterey Jack cheese for garnish

Heat oil in a small skillet. Cook onion over low heat for 6 to 8 minutes until soft and translucent. Add garlic, chiles, cumin and oregano. Cook for 2 minutes until spices release their fragrance. Place corn, green chiles and chicken broth in a medium stockpot, add onion mixture and bring to a boil. Lower heat and simmer for 15 minutes. Puree 1 can of the beans with a food processor. Add to stockpot with remaining beans, turkey and jalapeño sauce. Bring to a boil, taste for seasoning and add salt and pepper. Serve in heated soup bowls, garnish with cilantro leaves and pass cheese.

VARIATION
Grill 4 large chicken or turkey sausages, about 1 lb., slice thinly and add to soup in place of turkey or chicken.

COOKING SEAFOOD DISHES WITH CHILES

Many fish have a delicate flavor, and it is easy to overpower them with spice and chiles. We have tried to be moderate in our use of hot chiles in most of these dishes.

The distinctively flavored small Thai chile tends to be fiery hot. If you wish, substitute one or two serrano or two jalapeño chiles in its place in *Island Seafood Curry* or *Thai Shrimp Pizza*.

Scallop Risotto, with its piquant garlic, lemon and parsley overtones, makes a delicious first course as well as an entrée. The tiny, frozen ¾-inch bay scallops work well in this dish.

Grilling is one of the best ways to prepare fish. Recipes are included for *Grilled Shrimp in the Shell* with a spicy roasted garlic and sriracha sauce marinade, and *Moroccan Grilled Fish* with a spicy marinade made with hot Hungarian paprika. Grilled tuna is served with a somewhat spicy traditional wasabi and soy dipping sauce, and it is equally good with spicy Moroccan marinade.

Make *Jambalaya* with spicy shrimp and sausages for your next party. Try to get some New Orleans-style andouille sausage if you can. *Crab Enchiladas* can use surimi (imitation crabmeat) in place of more expensive crabmeat, for a very acceptable substitute. These can be assembled ahead of time and baked when you are ready to serve. *Tomatillo Salsa*, page 151, is a perfect accent for the enchiladas.

CRAB ENCHILADAS

Makes 6

If crabmeat is unavailable or very expensive, try surimi (imitation crabmeat) in these enchiladas. Other cooked fish or small salad shrimp would also be delicious. Cook and serve these in individual gratin dishes for a special presentation.

6 green onions, white part only, thinly sliced
1 tsp. vegetable oil
3 oz. light cream cheese, softened
2/3 cup sour cream
1/2 cup clam juice
8 oz. crabmeat or imitation crab, cut into 1/2-inch cubes
1 cup coarsely grated Monterey Jack cheese
2/3 cup roasted, diced green chiles, or 1 can (7 oz.),
   drained
2 tbs. finely chopped fresh parsley
1/2 tsp. Tabasco Jalapeño Sauce
salt and freshly ground pepper
1/4 cup milk
6 fresh corn tortillas
Tomatillo Salsa, page 151
cherry tomatoes for garnish

Preheat oven to 400°. Sauté green onions in vegetable oil for 3 to 4 minutes until soft. In a bowl, whisk together cream cheese, sour cream and clam juice until smooth. Remove ½ cup and reserve for enchilada topping. Add crabmeat, onions, Monterey Jack cheese, chiles, parsley and Tabasco to remaining sour cream mixture; mix well. Taste and adjust seasonings.

Beat ¼ cup milk into reserved sour cream mixture. Warm and soften tortillas by heating each side for 10 to 15 seconds in a medium-hot nonstick skillet. Spray a baking dish large enough to hold enchiladas in a single layer, or gratin dishes, with nonstick cooking spray. Spread about ⅓ of the sour cream mixture in baking dish. Spoon ⅙ of the crab mixture into each softened tortilla, roll up cigar-style and place seam- side down in baking dish. Spread reserved sour cream mixture over enchiladas.

Bake for 20 to 25 minutes, until topping is bubbling and lightly browned. Spoon a little *Tomatillo Salsa* over enchiladas. Garnish with cherry tomatoes.

CALAMARI RICE SALAD

Serve this salad for a summer lunch or as part of a buffet table. Some markets have cleaned squid available, or you may find frozen calamari rings in the supermarket freezer case. Make this ahead and chill for 2 to 3 hours before serving.

½ lb. cleaned calamari, cut into ½-inch rings
3 tbs. olive oil
4 green onions, white part only, finely chopped
2 tbs. finely chopped fresh green or red chiles
1 tsp. dried oregano
3 cups cooked long-grain rice

2 tbs. rice vinegar
grated peel (zest) from 1 lemon
2 tbs. lemon juice
1 tbs. capers
salt and freshly ground pepper
⅓ cup diced roasted red pepper
¼ cup coarsely chopped pitted kalamata or niçoise olives
¼ cup finely chopped fresh parsley

Thaw calamari if frozen. Prepare a bowl of ice water. Bring a pot of water to a boil and submerge calamari rings for 30 seconds. Immediately remove and plunge into ice water to stop cooking. Heat olive oil in a small skillet and sauté onions and chiles for 3 to 4 minutes, until softened. Add oregano and cook for 1 minute. In a large bowl, toss rice with hot onion mixture and add remaining ingredients and drained calamari. Chill salad before serving.

GRILLED SHRIMP IN THE SHELL

Servings: 2-3

Grilling shrimp in their shells helps keep the meat juicy and adds a little extra flavor. Choose large or even jumbo shrimp for this preparation and there will be fewer shrimp to clean. Cook shrimp on presoaked skewers or on a grill screen so they don't fall into the fire.

1 lb. large shrimp
2 tbs. lime juice
2 tbs. olive oil
½ tsp. sriracha sauce (see page 10)

5 cloves roasted garlic, page 19
salt and freshly ground pepper

Remove legs from shrimp, cut shrimp shells down the back with a sharp pair of scissors or a paring knife and pull out vein. Rinse and pat dry. In a small bowl, combine remaining ingredients to make a fairly smooth paste. Spread shrimp shells slightly away from shrimp bodies and spoon a little of the marinade into the indentation where the veins were removed; work mixture between shrimp body and shell. Cover and marinate in the refrigerator for 1 to 2 hours before grilling. Grill shrimp on a preheated grill for about 3 to 4 minutes each side, until shells turn pink and shrimp are firm to the touch. Serve hot.

ROASTED TOMATO, CHILE AND SHRIMP PASTA

Servings: 2

This flavorful pasta sauce includes blackened or roasted plum tomatoes which are cooked under the broiler or on the grill at the same time the chiles are roasted for peeling. If broiling, use a foil-lined baking sheet for easy cleanup. The roasting can be done hours or a day ahead. Radiatore, farfalle (bowties) or orecchiette pasta shapes are great in this dish.

4 plum (roma) tomatoes
1 poblano chile
1 jalapeño chile
6 oz. dried pasta
1 tbs. salt for pasta water
2 tbs. full-flavored olive oil
⅓ cup chopped red onion
1 clove garlic, minced
⅓ cup chicken broth
salt and freshly ground pepper
½ lb. shrimp, peeled, deveined
2 tbs. chopped cilantro for garnish

Heat broiler or grill and roast tomatoes and poblano chile, turning so all sides are browned and blistered. Remove from heat, cool slightly and remove tomato cores and poblano skin. Coarsely chop tomatoes, including some of the blackened skin for flavor, and reserve in a small dish. Dice poblano and jalapeño chiles.

Bring 3 to 4 quarts water to a boil, add salt and cook pasta. While pasta is cooking, heat olive oil in a large skillet and sauté onion for 3 to 4 minutes until softened. Add garlic, chiles, tomatoes, chicken broth, salt and pepper. Bring to a boil, add shrimp and cook for 1 to 2 minutes, until shrimp just turns pink. Drain pasta and add to skillet. Toss with shrimp sauce, add cilantro and serve immediately in warm bowls or plates.

THAI SHRIMP PIZZA

Makes two 11-inch pizzas

This savory pizza can be done from start to finish in 1 hour. A food processor makes quick work of the crust, or you could use a partially baked one from the market. The Thai chiles are extremely hot, so use care when handling. One little chile will flavor a whole pizza! Cut topping recipe in half if you only want to make 1 pizza. Brush the other pizza crust with a little olive oil, sprinkle with salt and bake as a flatbread, or top with a more traditional topping.

CRUST

1 cup warm water
1 tsp. brown sugar
1 pkg. active dry yeast

2 tbs. olive oil
3 cups all-purpose flour
3/4 tsp. salt

Preheat oven to 450° and preheat pizza stone, if using. Add water, sugar and yeast to food processor bowl. Pulse once or twice to mix. Add remaining ingredients and process until dough forms a ball. Dough will be quite soft. Remove from bowl, place on a floured board and knead a few times. Form dough into 2 equal balls. Cover each with plastic wrap and allow dough to relax for 5 minutes. Roll out dough into 10- to 12-inch circles. Place each on a piece of foil.

TOPPING

½ lb. medium shrimp, peeled, deveined, cut in half lengthwise

1 tbs. olive oil

1 large onion, cut in half through stem, thinly sliced

1½ tbs. finely chopped fresh red or green chile, or 1 small Thai chile, stemmed, finely chopped

2 cups finely shredded napa cabbage

2 tbs. Thai fish sauce (nam pla)

2 cups coarsely grated mozzarella cheese

2 medium-sized ripe tomatoes, peeled, seeded, chopped

12-15 fresh basil leaves, cut into thin ribbons

In a small pot of boiling salted water, blanch shrimp for 30 seconds, quickly drain and rinse under cold water to stop cooking. Drain and pat dry.

Place olive oil in a large skillet over medium heat. Add onion and chile and cook over low heat until onion is soft and translucent, about 10 minutes. Increase heat to medium-high, add cabbage, stir to combine and cook until cabbage just wilts. Add fish sauce and continue to cook until most of the liquid has evaporated.

To assemble: Distribute mozzarella evenly over dough, add cabbage mixture and top with shrimp. Bake pizzas on a pizza stone or baking sheet for about 12 to 15 minutes, until crust is nicely browned. If using a baking sheet, bake on the lowest oven shelf. Remove from oven, top with tomatoes and basil and cut into slices to serve.

SHRIMP JAMBALAYA

This savory Southern specialty makes a satisfying cold-weather supper or party dish. Add some leftover chicken or pork in place of the shrimp for a variation. Serve with a crisp green salad and hot bread.

6 thick slices smoked bacon, about ¼ lb., cut into 1-inch squares
3 cups chopped onions
½ cup chopped green bell pepper
½ cup finely chopped celery
1 tbs. finely diced cayenne or other fresh hot red chile
2 cloves garlic, finely chopped
3 tbs. finely chopped fresh parsley
1 cup diced Black Forest or other smoked ham
½ lb. andouille or Polish sausage, cut into ½-inch cubes
2 cups long-grain rice
4-4½ cups chicken broth
salt and freshly ground pepper
½ tsp. Tabasco Sauce
1½ lb. uncooked medium shrimp, peeled, deveined

Preheat oven to 350°. In a heavy ovenproof casserole, sauté bacon pieces until limp but not crisp. Remove bacon, leaving fat in pan. Add onions, green pepper, celery and chile. Sauté over medium heat for about 10 minutes until onions become translucent and vegetables soften. Add garlic and parsley; cook for 1 to 2 minutes, and add ham and sausage. Continue to cook until meats are hot. Pour in rice, stirring to mix well. Add reserved bacon, chicken broth, salt, pepper and Tabasco. Bring to a boil, stir well, cover tightly and place in oven. Stir mixture every 10 minutes or so, and add more broth or water if rice becomes too dry. After 20 minutes, stir in shrimp and return to oven. In 10 minutes stir again and taste a grain of rice for doneness. Adjust salt and pepper if needed. Add as much additional Tabasco as you like.

VARIATION

Add 1 cup chopped tomatoes, either canned and drained, or peeled, seeded fresh tomatoes, when you add the chicken broth. Reduce chicken broth by 1/2 cup.

ISLAND SEAFOOD CURRY

Servings: 4

This flavorful curry is served over rice. Choose a firm-fleshed fish such as swordfish, halibut, red snapper or shrimp. The Thai chile makes it very spicy, so you may wish to substitute a jalapeño or serrano chile.

2 tbs. butter
5-6 green onions, white part only, thinly sliced
4 cloves garlic, finely chopped
1 Thai or cayenne chile, stemmed, finely chopped
1 tsp. sambal oelek (see page 10)
1 tbs. Thai fish sauce (nam pla)

1 can (13½ oz.) unsweetened coconut milk
1 lb. fresh fish, cut into ¾-inch chunks
1 tbs. cornstarch
2 tbs. fresh lime juice
12-16 fresh basil leaves, cut into ribbons
8-10 fresh mint leaves, cut into ribbons
salt and freshly ground pepper
steamed rice

Heat butter in a large skillet; add onions, garlic, chile and sambal oelek. Cook over low heat for 2 to 3 minutes without browning garlic. Pour in fish sauce and coconut milk and bring to a boil. Add fish, reduce heat and cook over low heat for 4 to 5 minutes until fish flakes. Dissolve cornstarch in lime juice, bring liquid back to a low boil, add cornstarch mixture and cook until sauce thickens. Stir in fresh basil and mint leaves. Add seasoning. Serve over hot steamed rice.

MOROCCAN GRILLED FISH

Servings: 6

Try this spicy marinade on firm-fleshed fish or shellfish such as halibut, red snapper, tuna or shrimp. Serve with rice pilaf and sliced orange and red onion salad.

MARINADE

½ cup full-flavored olive oil
¼ cup lemon juice
2 cloves garlic, finely chopped
½ tsp. hot Hungarian paprika or New Mexico chile powder
½ tsp. Tabasco Jalapeño Sauce

2 tsp. ground cumin
¼ tsp. ground ginger
2 tbs. finely chopped fresh parsley
2 tbs. finely chopped cilantro
1 tbs. finely chopped fresh mint
salt and freshly ground pepper

2½-3 lb. firm-fleshed fish, about ¾-inch-thick fillets

Combine marinade ingredients in a small bowl. Place fish in a locking plastic bag and pour all but ¼ cup of the marinade over fish. Close bag, excluding as much air as possible, and refrigerate for 3 to 4 hours, turning bag occasionally. Remove fish from refrigerator about 30 minutes before grilling.

Preheat grill. Remove fish from marinade and discard this marinade. Grill fish for about 4 or 5 minutes each side, turning once, until fish is opaque and firm to the touch. Spoon a little of the reserved unused marinade over hot fish and serve.

SCALLOP RISOTTO

Servings: 4 as entrée, 6-8 as appetizer

A seafood risotto makes an elegant first course or main course. Substitute shrimp or crab for a delicious variation. Be sure to use Italian Arborio or another short-grain rice for a creamy texture.

2 cups chicken broth
1 cup clam juice
1 cup water
½ cup dry white wine
2 tbs. butter
2 tbs. olive oil
½ cup finely chopped onion
1 tbs. finely chopped fresh red or green chile
⅛ tsp. red pepper flakes
1½ cups Arborio or Silver Pearl short-grain rice
⅔ lb. small bay scallops, thawed if frozen, side muscle removed
salt and freshly ground pepper
3-4 cloves garlic, finely chopped
grated peel (zest) from 1 lemon
2 tbs. lemon juice
3 tbs. finely chopped fresh parsley

Combine chicken broth, clam juice, water and white wine in a saucepan and bring to a simmer. Heat butter and oil in a heavy 2- or 3-quart saucepan and sauté onion, chopped chile and red pepper flakes for 5 to 6 minutes until soft. Add rice, stir to coat with butter and oil mixture, and cook for 1 to 2 minutes until rice starts to turn translucent. Add about 1 cup of the hot broth mixture to rice and cook, stirring over medium heat until broth is absorbed. Continue to add broth, about $\frac{1}{2}$ cup each time, stirring until rice has absorbed liquid before adding more. The rice should remain at a simmer. Cooking over high heat does not shorten cooking time. After rice has cooked for a total of 15 minutes, bite into a grain of rice. It should be almost cooked through with just a small firm center. Add scallops, salt and pepper. Continue to cook for about 5 minutes, or until scallops are cooked. Stir in garlic, lemon peel, lemon juice and parsley. Serve immediately in a heated serving bowl or on warm plates.

NOTE: Depending on how high the heat was when cooking the risotto, there may be a little broth left over after risotto is perfectly cooked.

SEARED TUNA WITH
WASABI-CHILE DIPPING SAUCE

Servings: 4

Use only the highest quality sashimi-grade tuna, either fresh or frozen, for this dish. A good fish market or Japanese market is the best source for this grade tuna. Wasabi, powdered Japanese horseradish, comes in small cans and can be stored indefinitely on the shelf. Prepared wasabi is also available in a tube. Serve with steamed rice and a sliced tomato, cucumber and red onion salad.

DIPPING SAUCE

1/4 cup Japanese soy sauce
1 tbs. rice vinegar
1 jalapeño chile, stemmed, minced
1 tsp. peeled, finely grated ginger root
2 tbs. brown sugar, packed
1/4 tsp. powdered wasabi, or 1/2 tsp. prepared wasabi

4 tuna steaks, about 1 inch thick, 6-8 oz. each, lightly brushed with oil

Combine dipping sauce ingredients in a small bowl, stirring to dissolve wasabi powder. Set aside. Sear tuna on both sides over very hot coals or grill, or in a very hot cast iron skillet. Do not cook through. The interior of the steaks should be warm but should not change color from red to gray. Serve immediately on warm plates. Pour dipping sauce into individual dishes and serve with tuna.

VARIATION

Marinate tuna for 30 minutes in *Moroccan Grilled Fish* marinade, page 49, and grill. Spoon unused marinade over seared fish.

COOKING MEAT DISHES WITH CHILES

There are probably thousands of recipes for chili, the well known and loved meat and bean melange. We have limited this book to two, a traditional one with beef and a *Turkey and White Bean Chili*, in favor of including other equally spicy and delicious entrées.

Pork and chiles make a flavorful combination. Try *Chile Verde* with loads of green chiles and pork pieces that cook into a spicy and creamy filling for tortillas. For a dinner party entrée, make *Pepper-Stuffed Pork Loin* with its tunnel of colorful and flavorful bell peppers, onions and other vegetables, or *Roast Pork With Chile Crust*. There is a also a quick *Pork and Pepper Stir-Fry.*

Chorizo is sometimes hard to find in the market, so here is an easy recipe for making your own.

Grilled Lamb Steaks are coated with a chipotle-flavored dry rub for a quick dinner entrée. Spicy lamb pasta sauce reminds you of a traditional Italian-style restaurant dish, best eaten on a cold winter night with a glass of red wine. *Spicy Moroccan Grilled Sausages* are stuffed into pita pockets and served with a cooling yogurt sauce.

Grilled steak is featured in *Thai Steak Salad*, and with *Chimichurri Sauce*. *Chile Cheese-Stuffed Hamburgers* make a flavorful and juicy lunch or supper. Serve them with *Roasted Potato Wedges*, page 110, and some sliced tomatoes.

Try some of these robust chile-flavored entrées.

CHILI

Hearty beef chili makes a great winter lunch or supper. Some meat markets sell a coarsely ground chili meat which has been ground once through the chili plate of a commercial grinder. Shin beef is well worth seeking out. It has a high gelatin content and distinctive flavor. Taste for seasoning and add more chile powder, cayenne or liquid pepper sauce if you like a spicier chili. Chili is better when allowed to cool and reheated just before serving. Remove some of the congealed fat before serving. The fat carries much of the flavor, so do not remove it all. Leave more fat if you plan to thicken the chile. If you prefer a thicker chili, thicken the liquid with a little masa harina or cream of rice cereal. Serve it with beans or over fluffy rice.

3 lb. chuck or shin beef, coarsely ground
1 can (14½ oz.) beef broth
1 can (14½ oz.) redi-cut tomatoes
⅔ cup full-bodied beer or ale
½ cup dry red wine
1 large yellow onion, peeled, chopped
3 cloves garlic, minced

3 tbs. ground cumin
1 tbs. pure medium-hot chile powder
   (see page 11)
1 tsp. hot dry mustard
½ tsp. freshly ground pepper
2 bay leaves
2 tsp. salt

In a large skillet, lightly brown beef in several batches. Transfer meat to a Dutch oven or large heavy pot. Reserve about 2 tbs. fat in skillet. Add beef broth, tomatoes, beer and wine to meat in Dutch oven; bring to a simmer over low heat.

Add onion and garlic to reserved fat in skillet and cook over low heat for 8 to 10 minutes until onions are translucent but not brown. Add cumin, chile powder and mustard and cook for 2 to 3 minutes. Add onion mixture to beef with pepper and bay leaves. Simmer slowly for 1½ hours. Stir in salt. If possible, cool and reheat before serving.

CHILE VERDE

Servings: 8

This hearty dish can be served as a stew with hot tortillas, over rice or pasta, or as a burrito filling, topped with a little grated cheese. This is even better when made a day ahead so the flavors have time to blend. It also freezes well.

2½ lb. boneless pork butt
6 cups chicken broth
1½ cups chopped onions
5-6 cloves garlic, chopped
1½ tsp. salt
1 tsp. freshly ground pepper
2 bay leaves

3 lb. green Anaheim chiles, roasted and
   peeled, or 1 can (27 oz.) whole green
   chiles, stemmed and seeded
1 cup chopped peeled, seeded tomatoes
½ cup diced green or red bell pepper
1 tsp. dried oregano
¼ cup chopped cilantro leaves

Remove most of the fat from pork and cut into 1-inch cubes. Place in a large saucepan, cover with broth and bring to a boil. Skim off any surface scum. Add onions, garlic, salt, pepper and bay leaves. Lower heat, cover and simmer for about 1 hour, or until meat is almost tender. Coarsely chop chiles. Add chiles and remaining ingredients to pork, cover and simmer for 20 minutes, or until meat is very tender. Taste and adjust seasonings.

CHORIZO SAUSAGE

Makes 1 lb.

*Make this spicy Mexican sausage into patties, or crumble it into a hot skillet. Use it in **Chorizo Rice Casserole**, page 60, or roll some up in a tortilla with scrambled eggs, fresh salsa and a little grated cheese to make a breakfast burrito. It goes well in tacos and quesadillas, too.*

1 lb. coarsely ground pork
1 large clove garlic, minced
1 small fresh green or red chile,
   minced, optional
1½ tsp. ground cumin

½ tsp. New Mexico chile powder
¼ tsp. ground coriander
3 tbs. red wine vinegar
¼ tsp. salt
freshly ground pepper

Place meat in a large bowl, add remaining ingredients and mix well. Cover and refrigerate for several hours or overnight to allow flavors to blend. Form into 4 patties or crumble sausage into a preheated large skillet. Cook over medium heat until sausage is cooked through and lightly browned. Drain on paper towels.

CHORIZO RICE CASSEROLE

Servings: 4

Serve this savory rice casserole with a crisp green salad or sliced tomatoes and some hot bread for dinner. For a variation, make this dish with hot Italian sausages.

1 recipe *Chorizo Sausage*, uncooked,
    page 59
1 small onion, finely chopped
1/4 cup finely chopped celery
1 small fresh green or red chile, finely
    chopped
1 large tomato, peeled, seeded, chopped

4 cups cooked long-grain rice
1/2 cup coarsely grated Monterey Jack
    cheese
salt and freshly ground pepper
3/4 cup sour cream
1/4 cup chopped fresh parsley

Preheat oven to 375°. In a medium skillet, crumble chorizo and cook over medium heat, stirring frequently. Break up large pieces of sausage with a spatula. Sauté until sausage is cooked through and lightly browned. Remove sausage from skillet with a slotted spoon and reserve. Pour out all but 2 tbs. fat. Add onion, celery and chile to skillet, and cook until onion and celery are soft but not brown. Add tomato and cook for about 5 minutes, until tomato pieces release juice. Stir in rice, cheese, salt, pepper, sour cream and parsley. Place in a well buttered casserole. Bake for about 20 minutes, until rice is heated through.

CHILE-CHEESE STUFFED HAMBURGERS

Servings: 3

Spicy chiles and cheddar cheese make a juicy grilled hamburger.

1 lb. ground round
½ tsp. *Chipotle Puree*, page 19
1 roasted green chile, peeled, seeded,
  chopped, or use canned
salt and freshly ground pepper

6 tbs. coarsely grated extra-sharp
  cheddar cheese
3 hamburger buns
sliced tomato, onion and lettuce for
  garnish

Preheat grill. Mix ground meat with *Chipotle Puree*, chile, salt and pepper and form into 6 thin patties about 3½ inches in diameter. Place grated cheese in the center of 3 patties, leaving a ½-inch border. Top each with another patty and press edges together to seal in cheese. Grill to desired doneness and serve immediately on toasted buns with hamburger garnishes.

VARIATION

- Use 6 tbs. coarsely grated hot pepper Jack cheese instead of green chile and cheddar cheese.
- Use 5-6 roasted garlic cloves mixed with 4-5 tbs. Roquefort or blue cheese and divide among 3 patties.

GRILLED STEAK WITH CHIMICHURRI SAUCE

Servings: 4-6

*Grilled flank steak is marinated and served with a spicy parsley sauce that is said to be a favorite of the gauchos in Argentina. If you love garlic, use more. Serve with baked potatoes or **Chiles and Rice**, page 99.*

CHIMICHURRI SAUCE

4 cloves garlic
1 cup tightly packed parsley leaves,
    finely chopped to yield ½ cup
¼ cup finely chopped red onion
1 tsp. dried oregano

2 serrano chiles, stemmed, seeded,
    finely chopped
¼ cup cider vinegar
⅓ cup olive oil
salt and freshly ground pepper

1 flank steak, about 2 lb.

Combine all sauce ingredients in a small bowl. Cover and refrigerate for 3 to 4 hours. Trim flank steak and brush on both sides with sauce. Marinate at room temperature for 45 minutes. Grill steak on a preheated grill for 4 to 6 minutes each side for medium-rare, turning once. Remove to a cutting board, cover with foil and let meat rest for 5 minutes. With the knife at a 45-degree angle, cut meat into thin slices across the grain. Arrange meat on a platter and spoon a little sauce over meat. Pass additional sauce.

LAMB RAGU FOR PASTA

Serve this hearty lamb sauce over penne or ziti pasta shapes for a satisfying cool weather dinner. This sauce may be made a day or two ahead, or frozen.

1 lb. ground lamb
1 medium onion, finely chopped
$1/2$ cup finely chopped fresh mushrooms
$1\frac{1}{2}$ tsp. red pepper flakes
3 cloves garlic, finely chopped
$1/2$ tsp. dried rosemary, crumbled
3 tbs. tomato paste

1 can ($14\frac{1}{2}$ oz.) beef broth
salt and freshly ground pepper, optional
1 lb. dried pasta, cooked per package
    directions
$1/4$ cup grated fresh Parmesan cheese
$1/4$ cup chopped Italian parsley

In a large nonstick skillet, sauté lamb, breaking it into small pieces with a spatula. Stir and cook over high heat until lightly browned. Remove lamb from skillet with a slotted spoon. Add onion, mushrooms and red pepper flakes. Cook over medium heat until mushrooms have released their liquid and onion is soft and translucent, about 5 to 7 minutes. Add garlic and cook for 1 minute. Add rosemary, tomato paste, lamb and broth to skillet. Bring to a boil, reduce heat and simmer gently for 20 to 30 minutes, until sauce thickens slightly. Stir frequently to break up pieces of lamb. Add salt and pepper if needed. Drain cooked pasta and add to skillet, stirring well to combine. Add cheese and parsley; serve in heated bowls. Pass additional Parmesan.

SPICY MOROCCAN GRILLED SAUSAGES

Makes 6 patties

Serve these flavorful lamb sausage patties in pita pockets with a cooling yogurt sauce, or as part of a mixed grill with chicken and other grilled meats. The spicy Moroccan hot pepper paste, harissa, is packaged in a small can or tube in Middle Eastern markets, or you can substitute sambal oelek (see page 10).

1 lb. lean ground lamb
1 egg white, lightly beaten
1 large clove garlic, finely chopped
2 green onions, white part only, finely chopped
1 jalapeño chile, stemmed, seeded, finely chopped

2 tbs. chopped fresh parsley
1 tbs. red wine vinegar
$\frac{1}{2}$ tsp. harissa (see page 10)
$\frac{1}{4}$ tsp. cinnamon
$\frac{1}{4}$ tsp. ground coriander
$\frac{1}{2}$ tsp. ground cumin
$\frac{1}{2}$ tsp. salt

Place lamb in a bowl and stir in egg white. Add remaining ingredients and mix well. Preheat grill. Form lamb mixture into 6 patties about $\frac{3}{4}$-inch thick and grill for 5 to 6 minutes each side, turning once. Lamb should be cooked through, but still juicy. Serve hot. These patties can also be pan-fried in a nonstick skillet with a thin film of vegetable oil.

YOGURT SAUCE

Make this sauce 1 to 2 hours ahead and refrigerate it so the flavors have a chance to blend.

1 cup plain yogurt
3 green onions, white part only, finely chopped
1 tbs. finely chopped fresh parsley
1 tbs. finely chopped fresh mint
1 tsp. ground cumin
1 tbs. rice vinegar
½ tsp. Tabasco Jalapeño Sauce
1 medium tomato, peeled, seeded, chopped
salt and generous amounts of white pepper

Combine ingredients in a small bowl. Cover and refrigerate until ready to serve.

GRILLED LAMB STEAKS

Servings: 4

This is a quick entrée that marinates while you make the salad and heat the grill. Double the dry rub ingredients and spread it on a butterflied leg of lamb if you want to grill a larger piece of meat.

MARINADE
2 tbs. olive oil
2 tbs. lime juice
2 cloves garlic, finely chopped
1 tsp. *Chipotle Puree*, page 19
1 tbs. sweet Hungarian paprika
salt and freshly ground pepper

2 slices leg of lamb, 12-14 oz. each, or 4 shoulder steaks

In a small bowl, combine marinade ingredients to make a paste. Spread on both sides of meat and marinate for 20 to 30 minutes, or refrigerate for several hours. Cook on a preheated grill for about 4 minutes each side, depending on thickness of meat, until desired state of doneness is reached. If grilling large slices, divide into serving portions.

SOUTHWESTERN-STYLE BRISKET OF BEEF

*Chiles and spices coat the meat under a blanket of tomatoes and onion slices. The leftovers make terrific sandwiches. Serve with **Polenta With Hot Pepper Cheese**, page 109, or rice.*

2 tbs. *Chipotle Puree*, page 19
2 tbs. finely chopped jalapeño or
    serrano chile, or mixture
4 cloves garlic, finely chopped
grated peel (zest) and juice of 1 lime
1/4 cup brown sugar, packed
2 tsp. ground cumin

1 tsp. dried oregano
1 tsp. salt
freshly ground pepper
1 beef brisket, about 3 lb., trimmed of fat
2 onions, about 1 lb., thinly sliced
2-3 fresh tomatoes, peeled, seeded,
    chopped, about 1 1/2 cups

Preheat oven to 350°. In a small bowl, combine *Chipotle Puree*, chiles, garlic, lime peel and juice, brown sugar, cumin, oregano, salt and pepper. Mix well and spread evenly over both sides of brisket. Place 1/2 of the onions in a casserole or heavy baking dish with a tight-fitting lid. Arrange brisket on top of onions. Top brisket with remaining onions and chopped tomatoes. Bake, tightly covered, for 3 to 3 1/2 hours, until meat is very tender. Remove meat from baking dish, slice thinly across the grain and arrange on a warm serving platter. Surround with onions, tomatoes and pan juices.

THAI STEAK SALAD

Grilled marinated flank steak is paired with cool greens and a spicy chile dressing. Thai fish sauce (nam pla), sriracha sauce and lemon grass are some typical Thai ingredients found in Asian markets or ethnic food sections. Romaine or other sturdy salad lettuces torn into bite-sized pieces work well in this dish. Serve for lunch or as a light summer supper with hot garlic bread or crunchy breadsticks.

1 flank steak, about 1-1½ lb., trimmed

MARINADE

2 tbs. vegetable oil
1-2 tsp. coarsely chopped Thai or
    cayenne chiles
1 clove garlic, minced

1 tbs. lime juice
1 tsp. brown
sugar
salt

SALAD

6-7 cups mixed salad greens
1½ cups peeled, seeded, thinly sliced
    cucumbers
2 medium tomatoes, peeled, seeded,
    sliced into thin wedges

1 small red onion, thinly sliced
8-10 fresh mint leaves, cut into thin
    ribbons
½ cup cilantro leaves

DRESSING

3 tbs. lime juice
2 tbs. Thai fish sauce (nam pla)
1 tbs. brown sugar
2 tsp. sriracha sauce (see page 10)

2 tsp. sesame oil
2 cloves garlic, peeled, chopped
1 tsp. peeled, grated ginger root
1 stalk lemon grass*, optional

Place flank steak in a ceramic dish or stainless steel pan. Combine marinade ingredients and pour over steak, coating both sides. Marinate at room temperature for about 1 hour. Preheat grill. Grill over high heat for 4 to 5 minutes each side, or until medium rare. Remove meat to a cutting board, cover with foil and rest for 10 minutes. With a knife at a 45-degree angle, cut thin slices across the grain.

Place salad ingredients in a large bowl and toss to combine. Refrigerate until ready to serve. Combine salad dressing ingredients with a food processor or blender and process for a few seconds until fairly smooth.

To serve, arrange greens on a large platter or individual plates. Top with strips of grilled steak and drizzle dressing over meat and greens.

*To prepare lemon grass, cut off bottom 5 to 6 inches of stalk and remove tough outer layers. Smash peeled piece of lemon grass with the back of a heavy knife, cut into small thin pieces and process with dressing ingredients.

SAVORY MEAT LOAF

Servings: 6

This classic meat loaf, using your favorite combination of ground meats, is accented with smoky chipotle chiles. You can substitute regular dried bread or cracker crumbs for the panko (Japanese breadcrumbs).

2 tbs. olive oil
1 cup chopped onion
1 small red Fresno chile, stemmed,
    seeded, minced
2 cloves garlic, minced
1/2 tsp. ground cumin
2 lb. ground meat (beef, veal, turkey, or
    mixture, including some pork)

1 egg, lightly beaten
1 tbs. *Chipotle Puree*, page 19
1/2 tsp. salt
freshly ground pepper
1/2 cup panko or dried bread or cracker
    crumbs
3 tbs. chopped fresh parsley
3 tbs. chopped cilantro

Heat oven to 375°. Heat olive oil in a medium skillet and sauté onion for 5 to 6 minutes until softened. Add chile, garlic and cumin; cook for 1 minute. Remove from heat and cool slightly. In a bowl, stir together ground meat, egg, *Chipotle Puree*, salt and pepper. Add onion, crumbs, parsley and cilantro. Place mixture in a loaf pan and bake for about 1 hour, until juices run clear or internal temperature reaches 180°.

PORK AND PEPPER STIR-FRY

Servings: 3-4

This dish has a Szechuan flavor. Shao Xing is Chinese rice wine. Serve this stir-fry with steamed rice.

4 tbs. vegetable oil
1 lb. mushrooms, thinly sliced
6 green onions, white part only, thinly sliced
1 tsp. peeled, minced ginger root
1 tbs. minced fresh green or red chile, stemmed, seeded
1 tsp. chile paste with garlic (see page 10)

12 oz. lean pork, cut into matchstick-sized strips
1 large red bell pepper, cut into thin strips
salt and freshly ground pepper
1/2 cup chicken broth
2 tbs. soy sauce
2 tsp. cornstarch dissolved in 2 tbs. Shao Xing rice wine or dry sherry

Place 2 tbs. of the vegetable oil in a large skillet over high heat. Stir-fry mushrooms for about 5 minutes, or until liquid evaporates and mushrooms are lightly browned. Remove mushrooms from skillet and set aside. Add remaining vegetable oil to skillet and stir-fry onions, ginger, chiles and chile paste with garlic for 30 seconds. Stir in pork and cook for 2 to 3 minutes until meat is no longer pink, but not brown. Stir in red pepper. Return mushrooms to skillet and season with salt and pepper. Add chicken broth and soy sauce and cook over high heat until sauce boils. Stir in dissolved cornstarch and cook until sauce thickens. Serve immediately.

PEPPER-STUFFED PORK LOIN

Servings: 6-8

Here is an elegant entrée for a special dinner party. The colorful vegetable stuffing roll should be made ahead and frozen, so it can be done days or even weeks before it is needed. After you have butterflied the pork loin, the frozen vegetables are firm enough to stay in place while the roast is rolled and tied.

1 Japanese eggplant, peeled, cut into 1/4-inch-thick rounds, or 1 medium zucchini, cut into 1/4-inch-thick rounds
3 tbs. full-flavored olive oil
4 green onions, white part and 2 inches of green, cut into 1/2-inch pieces
1 tbs. finely chopped fresh red or green chile
2 cloves garlic, finely chopped
1/2 tsp. dried oregano
salt and freshly ground pepper
1/3 cup diced roasted red or yellow bell pepper, page 17, in 1/2-inch squares
4-6 oven-roasted tomatoes, page 17, or sun-dried, cut into 1/2-inch chunks
4-6 fresh mint leaves, cut into thin ribbons
6-8 fresh basil leaves, cut into thin ribbons
3 lb. boneless center-cut pork loin roast, about 12 inches long
Roasted Tomato Sauce, page 74

72 COOKING MEAT DISHES WITH CHILES

In a large skillet over medium heat, sauté eggplant slices in olive oil until soft and lightly browned. Remove from skillet and reserve. Add onions and fresh chile; sauté for 6 to 8 minutes until onions are soft. Stir in garlic, oregano, salt and pepper and cook for 1 minute. Cool slightly. In a bowl, combine eggplant, onion mixture, roasted pepper, tomatoes, mint and basil; mix well. Lay a long piece of plastic wrap on the counter and spoon vegetables into a thin roll, about 12 inches long and 1 inch in diameter. Roll up tightly in the plastic, and then in foil, and place in the freezer until firm, at least 2 to 3 hours.

Preheat oven to 375°. Butterfly pork roast with a long knife by making a cut along the long side of the roast about in the middle. Cut through the roast to within 1 inch of the other side, or about the same width of the thickness of the roast, so the roast can be opened like a book. Season roast with salt and pepper. Unwrap vegetable stuffing and place in middle of roast. Bring up pork sides around stuffing to meet, but do not overlap. Tie roast with kitchen string at several intervals. Roast on a rack, fat side up, in a roasting pan until internal temperature reaches 160°. Remove from oven, cover with foil and rest for 20 minutes before carving. Serve with *Roasted Tomato Sauce*.

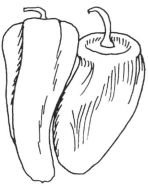

ROASTED TOMATO SAUCE

Makes 2 cups

This sauce can be done a day or two in advance, or on the morning of a party. The vegetables can be done a day or two ahead and refrigerated.

6 plum tomatoes, cored, quartered
salt and freshly ground pepper
1 medium onion, unpeeled, cut in half
olive oil
1 head garlic

2/3 cup chicken broth
1 tbs. full-flavored olive oil
2 tbs. red wine vinegar
salt and freshly ground pepper

Preheat oven to 250°. Line a baking sheet with foil. Place tomatoes on baking sheet cut-sides up. Sprinkle with salt and pepper. Brush cut sides of onion with olive oil and place cut-side down on baking sheet. Remove a few of the papery outside leaves of the garlic head, but do not peel. With a sharp knife, cut about 1/2-inch from top of garlic head. Drizzle cut top with olive oil, wrap in foil and place on baking sheet. Bake tomatoes for about 2 1/2 hours, until soft but not completely dry. Remove onion and garlic about 1 hour before tomatoes are done, or when they feel soft when pressed.

Remove peel from onion and discard. Place onion in a blender container. Squeeze out 4 of the roasted garlic cloves (reserve remaining cloves for another use) and place in blender container with tomatoes and remaining ingredients. Blend until smooth. Pour into a small saucepan, add salt and pepper, heat and serve with sliced pork.

ROAST PORK WITH CHILE CRUST

Servings: 6-8

*A boneless pork loin is partially roasted, topped with a spicy paste, and returned to the oven to finish cooking. Serve with baked potatoes and **Pepper Coleslaw**, page 108, or **Roasted Potato Wedges**, page 110, and a crisp green vegetable.*

2 dried New Mexico chiles, reconstituted
  (see page 20)
2 tbs. lime juice
1 tbs. vegetable oil
1 tbs. water
3 green onions, white part only,
  coarsely chopped

2 cloves garlic, coarsely chopped
2 quarter-sized pieces ginger root,
  peeled, coarsely chopped
1 small fresh red or green chile, minced
2 tbs. brown sugar, packed
2½-3 lb. boneless pork loin roast
salt and freshly ground pepper

When soft, remove chiles from soaking liquid; discard liquid. Place chiles in a blender container with remaining ingredients, except pork, and blend into a smooth paste. Preheat oven to 350°. Trim pork, rub with salt and pepper, place on a rack in a roasting pan and roast for about 30 minutes. Remove from oven. Spread dried chile paste over surface of roast. Return roast to oven and continue cooking until internal temperature reaches 160°, about 20 to 30 minutes. Remove roast from oven, cover with foil and rest for 20 minutes before carving.

PORK MOLE

Mole, a spicy pungent chile sauce, goes together quickly although it has a long ingredient list. This recipe makes 5 cups of sauce, more than needed for the pork, but mole keeps well and can be frozen for future use. Use the mole to moisten and sauce chicken enchiladas, over slices of cooked turkey or steak, or try a spoonful over scrambled eggs. The chocolate in the sauce will burn easily, so reheat the mole over very low heat, stirring constantly, or use the microwave. Serve with hot rice and a crisp green vegetable.

2 pork tenderloins, about 1¾ lb. total
salt and pepper
4 oz. dried chiles, including ancho,
    mulato, pasilla, guajillo, cascabel,
    reconstituted (see page 20)
3 tbs. vegetable oil
⅓ cup chopped onion
3 cloves garlic, chopped
2 cups chicken broth
1 cup chopped, peeled, seeded tomatoes
½ cup orange juice

½ cup blanched almonds
⅓ cup raisins
2 tbs. peanut butter
pinch cloves
½ tsp. ground fennel seed
½ tsp. ground coriander seed
salt and freshly ground pepper
1 round Mexican chocolate, about 3 oz.,
    coarsely chopped
fresh cilantro leaves for garnish
hot rice

Preheat oven to 350°. Trim pork tenderloins if needed, rub with salt and pepper and place on a rack in a roasting pan. Roast to 165°, about 45 to 50 minutes. Remove from oven and allow meat to rest.

Make sauce while meat is roasting. Tear reconstituted chiles into small pieces and place in a blender container. Heat 1 tbs. of the oil in a small skillet and sauté onion over medium heat for 4 to 5 minutes until soft. Add garlic and cook for 1 minute. Spoon onion and garlic into blender container. Add chicken broth, tomatoes, orange juice, almonds, raisins, peanut butter, cloves, fennel, coriander, salt and pepper. Process until mixture is very smooth, several minutes. Heat remaining oil in a large heavy sauté pan or saucepan over medium-low heat. Pour chile mixture into pan and cook, stirring constantly, until hot, but do not boil. Add chocolate and stir until it melts. With a knife at a 45-degree angle, slice pork into ½-inch-thick slices. Arrange on a warm serving platter or individual plates, add generous spoonfuls of mole, garnish with cilantro and serve with hot rice.

COOKING MEATLESS ENTRÉES WITH CHILES

In keeping with the trend towards eating less meat, many people are eating hearty vegetable main courses for lunch and dinner. Serve these delicious, filling entrées anytime, but they are particularly welcome during cooler weather.

Both *Potato Chile Soup* and spicy *Lentil Soup* are better the next day, so make them ahead and freeze them if you like. Serve *Potato Curry* with *Mango and Red Pepper Chutney*, page 154, or a fresh fruit salad. Pasta and rice always make satisfying entrées. Try *Spaghetti alla Puttanesca* with its full tomato, anchovy and black olive flavors, or make *Spicy Corn Risotto* with fresh or frozen corn. *Spicy Vegetable Gratin* with garbanzo beans makes a delicious main course after antipasto or salad.

POTATO CHILE SOUP

Serve this quick, creamy, mildly spicy pale green soup hot or chilled. Pass some **Tomatillo Salsa**, *page 151, to spoon into the soup and serve with crisp garlic bread.*

3 tbs. butter
1 large onion, thinly sliced
2 large leeks, white part only, washed
    well, thinly sliced
2 medium stalks celery, thinly sliced
4 cups thinly sliced potatoes, (3 large)
2-3 serrano chiles, stemmed, seeded,
    finely chopped

1 poblano chile, roasted, peeled,
    coarsely chopped
6 cups chicken broth
1 tsp. salt, or to taste
½ tsp. freshly ground pepper, or to
    taste
cilantro leaves for garnish

Melt butter in a large heavy pot. Sauté onion, leeks and celery for 5 to 6 minutes until softened. Add potatoes, chiles, chicken broth and salt. Bring to a boil, reduce heat, cover and simmer for about 20 minutes, until potatoes are tender. Cool for a few minutes and puree a small batch at a time with a blender or food processor until smooth. Add salt and pepper. Garnish with cilantro leaves and serve.

VARIATION

To 3 cups soup, add ½ cup cooked, diced ham or crumbled bacon and 1 cup whole kernel corn. Heat and serve.

LENTIL SOUP

Lentils are one of the easiest members of the legume family to use because they do not have to be presoaked, and they cook fairly quickly. They readily absorb the flavors of the foods and spices cooked with them. In this vegetarian soup, smoky canned chipotle chiles pureed with a little adobo sauce replace the traditional bacon or sausage. Serve with some hot crusty French bread. This soup can be refrigerated for a few days, or frozen.

1 lb. brown lentils
¼ cup olive oil
1 large onion, finely chopped
2 stalks celery, thinly sliced
2 medium carrots, thinly sliced
½ red bell pepper, finely chopped
2 jalapeño or serrano chiles, stemmed, seeded, finely chopped
4 cloves garlic, minced
1 tbs. *Chipotle Puree*, page 19

1 tsp. ground cumin
½ tsp. dried thyme
1 tsp. salt
½ tsp. freshly ground pepper
2 qt. water or vegetable broth
1 tbs. red wine vinegar
chopped fresh parsley for garnish

Pick over lentils to remove any little stones. Rinse with cold water and drain. Set aside. Heat olive oil in a 5- or 6-quart stockpot over medium heat; add onion, celery, carrots, red pepper, chiles and garlic. Cook for 5 to 6 minutes to soften vegetables. Add *Chipotle Puree*, cumin, thyme, salt, pepper, lentils and water. Bring to a boil, lower heat, cover and simmer gently until lentils are cooked through. Start testing lentils after 30 minutes. Most lentils will take about 45 minutes to cook, and some as much as 1 hour. When lentils are tender, stir in vinegar and adjust seasonings if necessary. Garnish with parsley and serve.

SPICY CORN RISOTTO

Servings: 4 as entrée, 6-8 as appetizer

This creamy rice dish is accented with bits of fresh hot chiles and fresh sweet corn kernels. Use Italian Arborio short-grain rice; California Silver Pearl rice makes an acceptable substitute. It will take about 20 minutes actual cooking time and, like pasta, should be served immediately.

4½ cups vegetable or chicken broth
2 tbs. butter
2 tbs. olive oil
½ cup finely chopped onion
2 cloves garlic, finely chopped
2-3 jalapeño or serrano chiles, stemmed, seeded, finely chopped
2 tsp. ground cumin
1½ cups Arborio rice
4 small tomatoes, peeled, seeded, chopped
1½ cups fresh or frozen, thawed corn kernels
1 tsp. salt
freshly ground pepper
2 tbs. chopped fresh Italian parsley
¼ cup grated Parmesan or manchego cheese

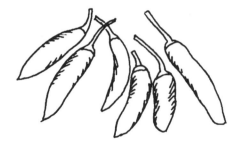

In a saucepan, bring broth to a simmer. Melt butter with oil in a heavy 2- to 3-quart saucepan and sauté onion for 5 to 6 minutes until soft. Add garlic, chiles and cumin, and cook for 1 to 2 minutes. Add rice, stir to coat with butter mixture and cook for 1 to 2 minutes until rice starts to turn translucent. Add about 1 cup of the hot broth to rice and cook, stirring, over low heat until broth is absorbed. Continue to add broth, about ½ cup each time, and stir until rice has absorbed all of the liquid before adding more. The rice should remain at a simmer. Cooking over high heat does not shorten cooking time. After rice has cooked for about 10 minutes, stir in chopped tomato pieces. After about 15 minutes, bite into a grain of rice. It should be almost cooked with just a small firm center. Add corn, salt and pepper. Continue to cook for 4 to 5 minutes to heat corn. Test rice again; if it is no longer has a firm center, stir in parsley and cheese. Serve in a heated bowl or on warm plates. Pass extra Parmesan cheese.

NOTE: Depending on how high the heat was when cooking the risotto, there may be a little broth left over after risotto is perfectly cooked.

SPAGHETTI WITH SPICY ITALIAN SAUCE (ALLA PUTTANESCA)

Servings: 4

This spicy classic sauce cooks in the time it takes the pasta water to boil and the pasta to cook. Since the pasta is the star here, make this dish with the best quality of imported Italian dried pasta available.

2 tbs. full-flavored olive oil
1/3 cup diced onion
2 tsp. minced jalapeño or serrano chile
4 cloves garlic, finely chopped
1/4 tsp. red pepper flakes
2 tbs. butter
1 can (14 oz.) tomato pieces, with juice
1/2 tsp. dried thyme
1 tbs. coarse salt for cooking water
12 oz. dried spaghetti

4-6 anchovy fillets, rinsed, drained and finely chopped
1/2 cup pitted, coarsely chopped kalamata olives
2 tbs. capers, drained
1/4 cup freshly grated Parmesan cheese
2 tbs. finely chopped fresh parsley
salt and freshly ground pepper

In a large pot, bring at least 6 qt. water to a boil over high heat. Heat olive oil in a large skillet and add onion and chile. Sauté for 3 to 4 minutes; add garlic and red pepper flakes. Cook over low heat for 1 to 2 minutes to soften garlic, but do not brown. Add butter, tomatoes and thyme, bring to a boil and cook over high heat for 4 to 5 minutes to thicken sauce. Reduce heat, stir in anchovies and simmer gently while pasta is cooking. Add 1 tbs. salt to boiling pasta water and add pasta. Stir pasta occasionally to keep strands from sticking together. When spaghetti has been cooking for 2 minutes less than the recommended package cooking time, test a strand of pasta by biting into it. The pasta should be cooked through, but firm to the bite (*al dente*). Drain pasta and add to skillet with olives, capers, cheese and parsley; toss to mix well. Add salt and pepper to taste. Serve immediately on heated plates. Pass extra Parmesan.

QUICK AND EASY SPICY PASTA

Servings: 2-3

This pasta sauce only takes 3 to 4 minutes to cook. Use your best olive oil and ripe flavorful tomatoes. Try capellini, linguine or spaghetti pasta.

2 tbs. full-flavored olive oil
3-4 garlic cloves, finely chopped
1-2 tbs. finely chopped fresh red or
   green chile
1 tbs. coarse salt for cooking water
8 oz. dried pasta, or 12 oz. fresh

3 large tomatoes, peeled, seeded,
   chopped
salt and freshly ground pepper
12-15 fresh basil leaves, cut into thin
   ribbons
½ cup grated Parmesan cheese

Bring at least 4 quarts water to a boil. Heat olive oil over low heat in a skillet large enough to hold cooked pasta. Cook garlic and chile for 3 to 4 minutes until softened but not brown. Add salt to boiling water and cook pasta until *al dente* (see page 85). Drain pasta, add to skillet and toss with garlic and chile. Add ½ of the tomatoes and season with salt and pepper. Toss and cook for 1 to 2 minutes. Add ½ of the basil leaves and all of the Parmesan cheese. Toss and pour into a warm serving dish or individual pasta bowls. Top pasta with remaining tomato and basil leaves. Pass additional cheese.

POTATO CURRY

Servings: 4

Serve this creamy, mildly spicy curry for lunch or supper with warm thick flour tortillas. It also makes a delicious side dish with grilled meats or roast chicken.

6 tbs. butter
1 large onion, peeled, chopped
2 red jalapeño chiles, stemmed, seeded, finely minced
2 green jalapeño chiles, stemmed, seeded, finely minced
2 large cloves garlic, finely chopped
1 tbs. curry powder

1½ lb. boiling potatoes, peeled, cut into 1-inch cubes
1 cup vegetable or chicken broth
1½ tsp. salt
freshly ground pepper
2 cups frozen green peas, thawed
½ cup coarsely chopped cilantro leaves

Melt butter in a large heavy saucepan. Add onion and chiles and cook over low heat until onion has softened and is translucent. Stir in garlic and cook for 1 minute. Add curry powder, stirring to combine, and cook for 1 to 2 minutes. Stir potatoes into curry mixture, add vegetable broth and bring to a boil. Cover pan, reduce heat and simmer for about 20 minutes, stirring occasionally. Test potatoes at 20 minutes, cooking for a few minutes longer if necessary until potatoes are tender. Add peas, bring mixture back to a boil and stir in cilantro. Serve immediately on warm plates or in small bowls.

SPICY VEGETABLE GRATIN

Summer vegetables are combined with garbanzo beans for a lightly piquant casserole. Sauté the eggplant in batches so it browns nicely. Serve this as part of a buffet, a side dish, or a main course with a crisp green salad and garlic bread.

1 large eggplant, about 1 lb.
1/4 cup full-flavored olive oil
1 1/2 cups chopped onions
4 large tomatoes, peeled, seeded, chopped
3 cloves garlic, finely chopped
1 tbs. finely chopped fresh chile
1 small red bell pepper, stemmed, seeded, cut into
    1/2-inch pieces
1/2 tsp. red pepper flakes
leaves from 2 sprigs fresh thyme
3 tbs. chopped fresh parsley
5-6 fresh mint leaves, cut into ribbons
1 can (15 oz.) garbanzo beans, rinsed and drained
salt and freshly ground pepper
1/2 cup grated Parmesan cheese

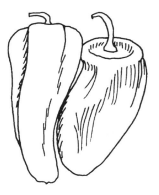

Preheat oven to 375°. Cut eggplant into ¾-inch slices, and then into ¾-inch cubes. In a large skillet, heat about 1½ tbs. of the olive oil. Over high heat, sauté ½ of the eggplant until lightly browned on all sides and soft, about 10 minutes. Stir frequently. Remove eggplant to a plate lined with paper towels. Add another 1½ tbs. of the oil to skillet and sauté remaining eggplant until lightly browned and soft. Remove to plate and drain. Add remaining oil and sauté onions over low heat for 5 to 6 minutes until onion softens. Increase heat to medium-high; add tomatoes, garlic, chile, red bell pepper, pepper flakes and thyme. Cook for 5 minutes to soften vegetables. Lightly oil a medium baking dish. Combine tomato mixture, eggplant, parsley, mint and beans. Season with salt and pepper. Pour into baking dish and sprinkle with Parmesan cheese. Bake, uncovered, for 30 minutes, or until vegetables are hot and nicely browned. Serve hot or at room temperature.

COOKING SIDE DISHES WITH CHILES

A wide array of lightly spiced vegetables and other side dishes are featured in this chapter. Serve these dishes with a main course or make two or three for an informal lunch or picnic fare. Many of them complement grilled fish, chicken or meat. *Chinese Fried Rice* or *Chile Corn Pancakes* could be served for for brunch. Take *Tomato-Stuffed Peppers*, *Pepper Coleslaw* or *Black Bean and Roasted Corn Salad* on a picnic.

Try *Easy Cowboy Beans*, *Black Bean and Quinoa Salad*, or *Spinach Salad with Cilantro Chile Vinaigrette* for your next cookout. Simple, nicely spiced vegetable accompaniments for a main course include *Broccoli with Ginger and Red Pepper Flakes* and *Roasted Potato Wedges*. *Polenta with Hot Pepper Cheese* is done in the microwave in under 15 minutes.

When you can get some nice eggplant at the market and have a little time to spend, make the Indian-spiced casserole, *Eggplant and Tomato Compote*. If the poblano chiles catch your eye, roast and stuff them with couscous.

Serve these spicy dishes with foods that are not so spicy, to avoid competing flavors in the meal.

BLACK BEAN AND QUINOA SALAD

Servings: 6-8

The Inca grain called quinoa is now grown in the high mountains of Colorado, so it is available in most supermarkets. Similar to rice both in cooking and taste, its volume triples as it cooks. Here quinoa is paired with black beans, some fresh chile and a spicy vinaigrette. Serve this salad in hollowed-out tomato shells, radicchio cups or on a platter lined with salad greens for a summer lunch or supper.

½ cup quinoa
1 cup water
salt
1 can (14½ oz.) black beans, rinsed
    and drained
⅓ cup diced roasted red bell pepper,
    page 17, or purchased
½ cup finely diced Monterey Jack or
    cheddar cheese
⅓ cup coarsely chopped cilantro

1 shallot, finely chopped
1 tbs. finely chopped fresh red or green
    chile
½ cup full-flavored olive oil
2 tbs. cider vinegar
2 tbs. lemon juice
1 tbs. Dijon mustard
1 tsp. sugar
salt and freshly ground pepper
cilantro leaves for garnish

Pick over quinoa carefully to remove any small stones or foreign matter. You can also remove the black unhulled grains if desired. Place quinoa in a bowl with cold water and drain through a sieve. Bring 1 cup water to a boil in a saucepan and add salt and quinoa. Lower heat, cover and simmer for 12 to 15 minutes, or until water has been absorbed and grains are tender. Remove from heat. Fluff with a fork and let stand covered for 5 to 10 minutes. Remove cover and cool, or refrigerate until ready to use.

Place black beans, roasted pepper pieces, cheese and cilantro in a bowl with quinoa. Combine shallot, chile and remaining ingredients, except cilantro, with a food processor. Process until well blended. Toss dressing with black bean mixture and serve. This can be made ahead and refrigerated. Remove from refrigerator about 30 minutes before serving. Garnish with cilantro.

BLACK BEAN AND ROASTED CORN SALAD

Servings: 6-8

Roasting fresh white or yellow sweet corn brings out its delicious toasty flavors. Serve this salad with grilled fish or meats, or with 2 or 3 other salads for a cool lunch or supper. To double the recipe, roast the corn in two pans so it cooks evenly. This keeps well for several days in the refrigerator.

3 large ears fresh tender corn
3 tbs. olive oil
salt and freshly ground pepper
1 can (15 oz.) black beans, rinsed and
    drained
1/2 cup diced roasted red bell pepper,
    page 17, or purchased
1/3 cup minced red onion

1/3 cup finely diced celery
1 tbs. minced fresh green or red chile
1 tsp. *Chipotle Puree*, page 19
1 tsp. dried oregano
1 tbs. lime juice
1 tbs. sherry vinegar
salt and freshly ground pepper
1/4 cup chopped cilantro leaves

Preheat oven to 425°. Cut kernels from corn cobs. Line a shallow rimmed baking sheet with foil. Toss corn with olive oil, salt and pepper, and spread out in a single layer on baking sheet. Bake for 15 to 18 minutes, stirring once or twice, until corn is lightly browned. Cool slightly and combine corn with remaining ingredients. Taste and add salt and pepper if needed. Refrigerate until ready to serve.

BROCCOLI WITH GINGER
AND RED PEPPER FLAKES

Try a little grated fresh ginger and a dash of red pepper flakes for a slightly piquant variation of cooked broccoli.

1 bunch broccoli, about 1 lb.
1 tbs. olive oil
1 clove garlic, chopped
$\frac{1}{2}$ tsp. peeled, finely chopped ginger root

$\frac{1}{4}$ tsp. red pepper flakes
salt and freshly ground pepper
$\frac{1}{2}$ cup water
1 tsp. sesame oil

Wash broccoli, cut off stem at base of florets, and divide florets so stalks are about thumb-size thickness. Cut off bottom 2 inches of stem and discard. Trim remaining piece of stem with a knife, removing about $\frac{1}{8}$-inch of outer peel. Cut trimmed stem into $\frac{1}{2}$-inch slices. In a large skillet with a lid, heat olive oil over high heat. Add broccoli florets and stem slices and cook for 1 to 2 minutes, coating broccoli with oil. Add garlic, ginger, red pepper flakes, salt and pepper, and stir to coat broccoli. Pour in water, cover pan and cook for 5 to 6 minutes, until broccoli is crisp-tender and water has evaporated. Remove from heat, drizzle with sesame oil and pour into a serving bowl. Serve hot or at room temperature.

EASY COWBOY BEANS

Servings: 6

Old West chuckwagons were almost always provisioned with beans, bacon and dried chiles. This recipe uses canned pinto beans, but if you have the time, beans cooked from scratch are better and less expensive. Serve with grilled meats.

2 dried pasilla or New Mexico chiles
4 strips thinly sliced smoked bacon, or 2 strips
    thickly sliced, cut into ½-inch pieces
1 small onion, chopped
1 tsp. ground cumin
2 cans (15 oz.) pinto beans with juice
½ tsp. hot dry mustard
salt and freshly ground pepper
2 tbs. brown sugar, packed
hot pepper sauce, optional

Rinse chiles briefly under running water and pull off stems. Cut open chiles and remove seeds. Heat a heavy skillet over medium heat and toast chile pieces for a few seconds on each side to soften. Do not burn. Place chiles in a small bowl and cover with boiling water. Soak for 20 minutes, drain, chop coarsely and puree with a blender or food processor. Add 1 to 2 tbs. water if mixture is too thick to make a paste.

Cook bacon in a heavy-bottomed saucepan until cooked through but not crisp. Remove bacon pieces with a slotted spoon and set aside. Pour off all but 1 to 2 tbs. bacon fat and add onion to pan. Cook over medium heat for 6 to 8 minutes until onion is translucent but not brown. Remove from heat and stir in cumin and pureed chiles. Return to heat and cook for 1 minute to bring out flavors.

Add beans, liquid, dry mustard, brown sugar and bacon to saucepan. Cook over low heat for 15 to 20 minutes, stirring frequently. Taste for salt and add a few drops of your favorite hot pepper sauce if desired.

CHINESE FRIED RICE

Servings: 4

This makes a good brunch or lunch dish. Serve with a platter of melon slices or fresh fruit salad. Cook extra long-grain rice and refrigerate or freeze the leftovers. Rice for fried rice needs to be cold.

4 cups cooked long-grain rice
3 tbs. vegetable oil
6 green onions, white part only, thinly sliced
1 small fresh red or green chile, stemmed, seeded, finely chopped
1/2 cup finely diced smoked ham

1 egg, lightly beaten
1/2 cup peas, defrosted if frozen
1/8 tsp. white pepper
1 tbs. Shao Xing rice wine or dry sherry
1 tbs. soy sauce
2 tbs. finely chopped fresh parsley

Pour rice out onto a large flat plate or platter and mash clumps of rice with your fingers to separate grains. Place a wok or large skillet over high heat, add vegetable oil and swirl to coat pan. Add onions, chile and ham and stir for 1 to 2 minutes. Pour in rice, stir to coat each grain with oil and cook for 3 to 4 minutes to heat through. Make a well in the middle of rice and add egg to well. Stir egg vigorously, and as it sets, stir into rice, leaving bits of cooked egg. Mix in peas and white pepper. Pour Shao Xing and soy sauce over rice and stir to combine. Garnish with parsley. Serve in a warm bowl, or mold in a small bowl and turn out onto heated plates.

CHILES AND RICE

Colorful hot chiles and roasted red peppers are combined in this flavorful side dish. Serve with roasted or grilled meats and hot French bread.

½ cup diced onion
2 tbs. vegetable oil
2 cloves garlic, minced
1½ tsp. minced serrano or jalapeño
    chile
1 tsp. ground cumin
1¼ cups long-grain rice

2½ cups hot water
1 tsp. salt
1 tsp. sriracha sauce (see page 10) or
    Tabasco Jalapeño Sauce
⅓ cup diced roasted red bell pepper,
    page 17 or purchased, or pimiento
3 tbs. coarsely chopped cilantro leaves

In a 1½-quart heavy saucepan, sauté onion in oil for 3 to 4 minutes until onion softens. Add garlic, chiles and cumin. Cook for another minute. Add rice, stirring to coat with onion and spice mixture, and cook for 2 to 3 minutes until grains turn slightly translucent. Add hot water, salt and sriracha sauce. Bring to a boil. Reduce heat to low, cover and simmer for 18 to 20 minutes, until all liquid is absorbed and rice is tender. Fluff with a fork and stir in pepper pieces and cilantro. Serve hot.

VARIATION

For a slightly richer-tasting dish, use chicken broth instead of water, and long-grained basmati rice.

CHINESE GREEN BEAN AND MUSHROOM STIR-FRY

A food processor makes quick work of finely chopping the onions, garlic, ginger, chile and mushrooms. Serve this as a vegetable side dish, or use ground pork instead of mushrooms, and serve it as an entrée with steamed rice.

4 green onions, white part only, minced
2 cloves garlic, minced
2 quarter-sized pieces peeled ginger root, minced
1 red Fresno chile, minced
½ lb. finely chopped mushrooms
1 tbs. *Hot Chile Oil*, page 162, or
    purchased chile oil
1 tbs. vegetable oil
1 lb. green beans, stemmed
½ cup water
2 tbs. soy sauce
1 tbs. Shao Xing rice wine or dry sherry
½ tsp. sesame oil

Combine onions, garlic, ginger root and chile with mushrooms and set aside for 15 minutes to blend flavors. Heat chile oil in a large skillet and add chopped mushroom mixture. Sauté for 2 to 3 minutes and remove from skillet. Add vegetable oil to skillet. Add green beans and stir to coat with oil; cook for 2 to 3 minutes. Add water to beans, cover and cook over high heat until liquid evaporates and beans are crisp-tender, about 4 to 5 minutes. Return mushrooms to skillet with beans, soy sauce, Shao Xing and sesame oil. Mix well and serve immediately.

VARIATION
Use 1/2 lb. ground pork instead of mushrooms. Sauté in chile oil, breaking pork into small pieces with a spatula, and cook to a light brown color. Remove pork from skillet with a slotted spoon and drain fat from skillet. Continue with recipe, returning pork to skillet when beans are crisp-tender.

CORN CHILE PANCAKES

Serve these for brunch or lunch with a fresh fruit salad, or to accompany a main dish. These can be made in small cocktail size and topped with a little smoked salmon and dilled sour cream, or some tomato salsa.

2 large eggs
1/4 cup sour cream
2 tbs. butter, melted
2 tbs. diced roasted, peeled poblano
    chile
2 tbs. diced roasted red bell pepper,
    page 17 or purchased, or pimiento

1 cup fresh corn kernels, about 3 ears
1/2 tsp. New Mexico chile powder
1/2 cup flour
1/2 tsp. baking powder
1/2 tsp. salt
freshly ground pepper
2 tbs. vegetable oil

In a large bowl, beat together eggs, sour cream and butter. Add remaining ingredients, except vegetable oil, and mix well. Heat vegetable oil in a skillet over medium heat. Spoon in batter about 2 tablespoons at a time, making 2- to 3-inch pancakes. Cook, turning once, until pancakes are lightly brown and firm to the touch. Serve immediately.

CORN AND CHILE PUDDING

Servings: 4

Make this when fresh corn is in season. The savory corn kernels and piquant chiles bake into a creamy side dish that is delicious with grilled or roasted chicken or pork. Or serve it as an entrée for two with a crisp green salad.

1 tbs. vegetable oil
1 cup finely chopped onion
1/2 cup diced red bell pepper
1-2 tsp. minced red Fresno or jalapeño chile
1 tsp. ground cumin
1/2 tsp. ground coriander
1/4 tsp. dried oregano

2 eggs
1/3 cup milk
1 cup corn kernels, about 3 ears
1/2 cup grated pepper Jack or cheddar cheese
1/2 tsp. baking powder
salt and freshly ground pepper

Preheat oven to 350°. Butter a 1-quart baking dish. Heat oil in a medium skillet and sauté onion, red pepper and chile for 8 to 10 minutes, until onion is soft and translucent. Add cumin, coriander and oregano to skillet and cook for 1 minute. Set mixture aside to cool slightly. In a bowl, whisk eggs until well combined. Add remaining ingredients and onion-chile mixture. Pour into baking dish and bake for 30 minutes, or until puffy and lightly browned around the edges. Serve immediately.

COUSCOUS-STUFFED POBLANO CHILES WITH ORANGE SAUCE

Serve these stuffed chiles with grilled fish, chicken or meat. Make them ahead and heat them in the oven just before serving.

4 fresh poblano chiles
1 tbs. butter
2 green onions, white part only, thinly sliced
1/2 tsp. ground cumin
1/2 cup water or chicken broth
1/3 cup quick-cooking couscous
1 tbs. raisins
1 tbs. pine nuts
salt and freshly ground pepper
Orange Sauce, follows

Roast chiles under a broiler until skin blisters and blackens. Remove from oven and cool. Pull off papery skin. Keep stems, but cut a thin slit in one side of each chile. Carefully pull out seeds and membrane. Pat chiles dry.

In a medium skillet, melt butter. Sauté onions for 2 to 3 minutes until soft; add cumin and cook for 1 minute. Add water, bring to a boil and stir in couscous, raisins, pine nuts and seasonings. Cover pan, remove from heat and let rest for 5 minutes. Fill chiles with couscous mixture and pull sides of chiles together to cover filling. Place in an ovenproof baking dish. When ready to serve, preheat oven to 400°. Bake uncovered for 10 to 12 minutes, until chiles and filling are hot. Spoon *Orange Sauce* over chiles and serve.

ORANGE SAUCE
grated peel (zest) from 1 orange
$1/3$ cup orange juice
salt and freshly ground pepper
4-5 drops Tabasco Jalapeño Sauce
1 tsp. cornstarch dissolved in $1/4$ cup chicken broth

Combine ingredients in a small saucepan. Bring to a boil and stir until sauce thickens. Serve over stuffed chiles.

EGGPLANT AND TOMATO COMPOTE

Servings: 4

Indian spices flavor this easy vegetable melange. Serve with grilled chicken or meat, or as a buffet dish.

2 dried ancho or New Mexico chiles
1 large eggplant, about 1¼ lb.
olive oil for brushing eggplant
1 tbs. finely chopped fresh red or green chile
1-inch piece ginger root, peeled, coarsely chopped
4 cloves garlic, peeled, coarsely chopped
1 tbs. olive oil
1 tsp. ground cumin
1 tsp. ground coriander
½ tsp. curry powder
pinch cinnamon
1 can (14½ oz.) tomato pieces with juice
1 tbs. cider vinegar
1 tbs. brown sugar, packed
salt and freshly ground pepper

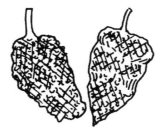

Rinse off dried chiles, discard stems, break open and discard seeds. Lightly toast chile pieces in a medium-hot skillet for a few seconds to soften. Place chile pieces in a small bowl, cover with boiling water and soak for 20 minutes. Preheat broiler. With a vegetable peeler, completely peel or remove alternate 1-inch sections of eggplant skin, giving a striped look. Cut eggplant into 1/2-inch slices, place on foil-lined baking sheets, lightly brush with oil and broil for 4 to 5 minutes, or until lightly browned. Turn slices over, brush with oil and broil for 3 to 4 minutes, until eggplant is soft and lightly browned. Remove from oven and stack cooked eggplant slices on top of each other, making 3 or 4 stacks. Fold foil over to cover eggplant and let it steam for a few minutes.

Drain chiles, reserving soaking water. If some pieces are still papery or leathery, cut into small pieces. Chop chiles coarsely, and place in a blender or food processor container with fresh chile, ginger, garlic and 1 tbs. of the soaking liquid or water. Process until mixture is finely chopped, adding 1-2 tbs. more liquid if necessary. Heat 1 tbs. olive oil in a large skillet and sauté chile mixture over low heat for 2 to 3 minutes. Add cumin, coriander, curry and cinnamon. Cook for 1 to 2 minutes until spices release their fragrance. Add tomatoes with juice, vinegar and brown sugar to skillet and bring to a boil. Cut cooked eggplant slices into quarters and add to skillet with salt and pepper. Mix well and cook for 15 to 20 minutes over low heat to blend flavors. Taste for seasoning, adding salt and pepper as needed. Serve warm.

PEPPER COLESLAW

Serve this zippy coleslaw with grilled fish, chicken or meat. Make it at least 3 to 4 hours ahead so flavors can develop. A food processor makes quick work of shredding cabbage and grating carrots —use the 1mm slicing blade for the cabbage, and the coarse shredding blade for the carrots. Use both red and yellow bell peppers for color, if you have them.

6 cups thinly sliced cabbage, about ½ large head
2 carrots, peeled, coarsely grated
½ red bell pepper and ½ yellow bell pepper, or 1 bell pepper
1 tbs. finely chopped fresh red or green chile

½ cup mayonnaise
¼ cup sour cream
1 tbs. Dijon mustard
3 tbs. cider vinegar
¼ tsp. sambal oelek (see page 10), optional
salt and freshly ground pepper

Place sliced cabbage and grated carrots in a large bowl. With a vegetable peeler, peel bell peppers, cut into quarters and cut each quarter in half horizontally. Cut each piece into thin strips and add to cabbage with chile. In a small bowl, whisk remaining ingredients until smooth. Pour over cabbage mixture and toss until well combined. Check seasoning, adding more salt and pepper if needed. Cover and refrigerate for 3 to 4 hours before serving.

MICROWAVE POLENTA
WITH HOT PEPPER CHEESE

Making polenta in the microwave is surprisingly easy and foolproof. Serve with grilled or roast chicken. Top with a spoonful of tomato sauce or fresh salsa if you like. Leftovers can be reheated in the microwave. Use a deep microwavable dish that will be less than half filled with the cornmeal water mixture, because it will bubble up during cooking.

1/2 cup polenta cornmeal
2 1/2 cups water
1/2 tsp. salt
1 tbs. butter, softened
2 oz. pepper Jack cheese, grated

Combine polenta, water and salt in a microwavable dish. Cook, uncovered, on HIGH for 5 to 6 minutes. Remove from microwave, stir, and cover with a vented plastic lid or paper towel. Return to microwave and cook for 5 to 6 minutes. Most of the liquid should have been absorbed by the cornmeal. Mixture will thicken as it cools, but if it is quite thin, cook for 1 additional minute. Stir in butter and cheese. Covered, this will keep warm for several minutes until you are ready to serve.

ROASTED POTATO WEDGES

These are better than French fries and much lower in fat.

2 large baking potatoes
2 tbs. full-flavored olive oil

1½-2 tsp. chile powder
salt and freshly ground pepper

Preheat oven to 400°. Cut potatoes in half lengthwise, and cut each half into 5 or 6 wedges. Line a shallow baking pan or jelly roll pan with foil. Pour olive oil on a plate or in a bowl and toss potato wedges in oil, making sure cut sides are moistened. Place wedges on baking sheet, peel side down. Combine chile powder with salt and pepper. Lightly sprinkle over potato wedges. Bake for about 35 minutes, or until lightly puffed and browned. Serve immediately.

VARIATIONS

- Combine olive oil, salt and pepper and toss with potato wedges. Lightly sprinkle ½-¾ tsp. red pepper flakes over potato wedges before baking.
- Combine olive oil, salt, pepper and 1 tsp. Tabasco Jalapeño Sauce. Toss with potato wedges and bake.
- Combine olive oil and 1½ tsp. *Chile Salt*, page 130. Toss with potato wedges and bake.

SPINACH SALAD WITH CILANTRO CHILE VINAIGRETTE

This piquant vinaigrette is a delicious dressing for a chicken or shrimp salad. Store unusued vinaigrette in the refrigerator.

VINAIGRETTE

3 tbs. rice vinegar
1 tbs. Dijon mustard
1 tsp. *Chipotle Puree*, page 19, or
   sriracha sauce (see page 10)

1 tsp. brown sugar
1/3 cup olive oil
3 tbs. minced cilantro leaves
salt and freshly ground pepper

1 lb. fresh small spinach leaves
roasted, salted pumpkin seeds (*pepitas*), toasted slivered almonds or chopped
   hard-cooked egg

Combine vinaigrette ingredients with a food processor or blender. Process until mixture is well blended. Wash and dry spinach leaves, removing long stems. Place in a salad bowl and toss with 3 to 4 tbs. of the vinaigrette, or enough to moisten. Sprinkle with pumpkin seeds, almonds or chopped egg. Serve immediately.

TOMATO-STUFFED PEPPERS

Servings: 4

Colorful bell peppers are stuffed with spicy tomato filling and topped with feta cheese. Serve warm or at room temperature with grilled fish or chicken.

2 large red or yellow bell peppers, quartered, or 4 small peppers, halved
2 tbs. olive oil
1/2 cup finely chopped onions
2 tbs. finely chopped fresh red or green chiles
2 cloves garlic, finely chopped
3 cups coarsely chopped peeled, seeded tomatoes

3 tbs. finely chopped fresh basil
leaves from 2 sprigs fresh thyme
salt and freshly ground pepper
1/4 cup crumbled feta cheese or
    Mexican *queso fresco* (fresh cheese)
cilantro leaves for garnish
small black olives for garnish

Parboil bell peppers for 3 to 4 minutes or microwave until peppers are slightly softened but still keep their shape. Heat oil in a medium skillet. Sauté onion and chiles for 5 to 6 minutes, until onion turns translucent. Add garlic and cook for 1 minute. Stir in tomatoes, basil, thyme, salt and pepper. Cook over medium-high heat for 8 to 10 minutes, until juices are absorbed and mixture is slightly thickened. Heat broiler. Spoon sauce into pepper pieces. Crumble cheese on peppers and broil to melt cheese. Garnish with cilantro and olives.

MAKING SMALL DISHES WITH CHILES FOR APPETIZERS AND SNACKS

Chile dishes make great party foods! This chapter is filled with many nicely spiced appetizer and first course-type dishes.

Try easy spicy *Pinto Bean Dip* with tortilla chips. Make some *Chile Lovers' Tortilla Chips* to dip in your own or purchased salsa. *Spicy Pecans* and *Hot Chile Peanuts* are great nibbles and keep well in an airtight container. Hot chiles and cheese are a great taste duo in *Chipotle Cheese Ball* or *Marinated Chile Goat Cheese*. *Chile Cheese Shortbread* can be served as an appetizer or informal cheese course with some red wine.

Soups make delicious first courses. Choose creamy *Cold Avocado Soup* or *Spicy Gazpacho* for a warm summer evening, and hot *Sweet Potato Soup* for a winter holiday dinner.

Other party favorites include chicken wings, *Chile Deviled Eggs* and *Spicy Mustard Shrimp*. Quesadillas, too, go together quickly and several can be baked at one time, cut into wedges and served with a salsa.

Serve some of these spicy small dishes for your next party.

CHILE CHEESE SHORTBREAD

This spicy shortbread is savory, not sweet. Serve these rich cheese squares with a glass of champagne or white wine, or with red wine as a cheese course. Make them ahead and store them in an airtight container, or freeze. Use a full-flavored extra-sharp cheddar cheese for the best flavor.

1 cup all-purpose flour
1/2 tsp. dry hot mustard
1/2 tsp. New Mexico or pasilla chile powder
1/4 tsp. ground cumin
1/4 tsp. salt

2 tbs. finely grated Parmesan cheese
4 oz. extra-sharp cheddar cheese, coarsely grated
1/2 cup cold unsalted butter, cut into 8-10 cubes

Place flour, mustard, chile powder, cumin, salt and Parmesan cheese in a food processor workbowl. Pulse a few times to combine. Add cheddar cheese and butter and pulse until mixture looks like coarse meal. Process only until dough forms a ball. Remove dough and pat into an 8-inch square baking pan. Smooth to an even thickness. Using fork tines, make a pattern in the soft dough, either straight lines or criss-crosses. Refrigerate for at least 1 hour.

Preheat oven to 325°. Bake for about 40 to 45 minutes, or until light brown. Remove from oven and cut into 36 squares. Place pan on a rack to cool.

CHILE CHEESE POPCORN TOPPING
Makes about ¼ cup

Looking for a hot and spicy popcorn flavoring? This is it. Increase the chile powder or add a pinch of cayenne pepper for more heat. This is also great on oven-baked corn tortilla chips. Oven-drying the cheese brings out more flavor, but this is optional. The Parmesan in the green can works well in this. Pop the corn in **Hot Chile Oil**, *page 162, or if you use an air popper or microwave, drizzle some chile oil over the hot popcorn before sprinkling with the topping.*

3 tbs. grated Parmesan cheese
2 tsp. Kosher salt
1 tsp. New Mexico or pasilla chile powder
1 tsp. ground cumin

½ tsp. hot dry mustard
1 tsp. onion powder
½ tsp. garlic powder
¼ tsp. finely ground white pepper

Preheat oven to 200° and turn off heat. Place cheese in a shallow cake pan and put into the oven to dry cheese, but not toast it. Stir occasionally. Allow oven to cool to room temperature, about 30 minutes. Place all ingredients in a spice grinder, food processor or blender container. Process on high until well combined and finely ground, approaching a powder. Pour into a small glass container with a tight lid. Sprinkle 1 to 2 tsp. over freshly popped corn.

CHILE DEVILED EGGS

Serve these piquant eggs as part of an antipasto platter, or with a salad or two for lunch or supper.

4 hard-cooked eggs
3 tbs. mayonnaise
2 tsp. Dijon mustard
1/2 tsp. Tabasco Jalapeño Sauce
1/4 tsp. dried oregano
1/2 tsp. ground cumin
1 tsp. finely minced serrano chile
salt and freshly ground pepper
2 tbs. finely chopped cilantro leaves
pimiento strips for garnish

Peel eggs and cut in half. Remove yolks to a small bowl and mash with a fork. Stir in mayonnaise, mustard and Jalapeño Sauce, mixing well. Add remaining ingredients, except pimiento, and combine. Divide mixture among egg white halves and garnish each with a small strip of pimiento. Refrigerate if not serving immediately.

CHILE- AND LIME-SPIKED FRUIT

Sweet slices of fresh summer fruit taste even sweeter with a sprinkle of chile powder and a squeeze of lime. Serve a platter of fruit for a pool party or barbecue, or for brunch. Each person can use chile powder and lime to taste.

fresh, ripe fruit: pineapple, melons, papaya, mango or peaches, cut into wedges or
    chunks
pure New Mexico or pasilla chile powder
limes
fresh mint leaves for garnish

Cut fruit into slices or chunks and arrange on plates or a platter. Either drizzle fruit with lime juice and dust with chile powder, or pass a plate of limes and a small bowl or shaker of chile powder.

VARIATION

Wrap chunks of seasoned fruit in thin strips of prosciutto before serving.

CHILE LOVERS' TORTILLA CHIPS

This is a perfect way to use up a few leftover corn tortillas when you make tacos or enchiladas.

Hot Chile Oil, page 162
corn tortillas
Chile Salt, page 130, optional
Chile Cheese Popcorn Topping, page 116, optional

Preheat oven to 325°. Using a pastry brush, apply a light coat of *Hot Chile Oil* on both sides of tortillas. Sprinkle lightly with *Chile Salt* or *Chile Cheese Popcorn Topping*. Cut each tortilla into 8 wedges and place on a baking sheet in a single layer. Bake until crisp and lightly brown, about 8 to 10 minutes. Turn off oven and allow chips to cool in oven with door ajar. When cool, store in an airtight container.

VARIATION
When chips are crisp, top with a little grated cheddar and place in a hot oven just long enough to melt the cheese. Garnish with thin rings of jalapeño chiles for perfect nachos.

CHIPOTLE CHEESE BALL

Makes one 4-inch ball

Make this ahead and keep it in the refrigerator for a quick appetizer or a cheese course with fruit. If you prefer, pack the cheese mixture into a small crock, and use as a spread on crackers or toasts. The cheese ball should be served at cool room temperature for easy spreading, so take it out of the refrigerator 1 hour before serving, or put it on a microwavable plate and warm it on the defrost cycle for 45 seconds to 1 minute.

½ lb. sharp cheddar cheese, coarsely grated, room temperature
3 tbs. butter, softened
2 tbs. grated Parmesan cheese
1 tsp. hot dry mustard
1½ tsp. *Chipotle Puree*, page 19
½ tsp. onion powder
½ cup coarsely chopped toasted pecans

Place all ingredients, except pecans, in a mixer bowl and beat until mixture is smooth. Remove cheese mixture with a spatula to a piece of waxed paper and place in the refrigerator for 30 to 45 minutes, until mixture can be formed into a ball. Roll ball in chopped pecans.

COLD AVOCADO SOUP

This elegant creamy soup makes a perfect starter for a hot summer night. Make it early in the morning, or at least 2 to 3 hours before serving, so it has a chance to chill thoroughly. Serve this in pretty glass bowls.

2 medium-sized ripe Haas avocados, peeled, seeded, coarsely chopped
2 cups chicken broth
1/2 cup heavy cream
3 tbs. lime juice
2 tsp. Tabasco Jalapeño Sauce
salt and white pepper
1 ripe tomato, peeled, seeded, chopped, for garnish
sour cream for garnish
chopped cilantro leaves for garnish

With a food processor or blender, puree avocados, chicken broth, cream, lime juice and Tabasco until very smooth. Check seasoning, adding salt and pepper if needed. Pour into a glass or stainless steel bowl, cover and refrigerate for 2 to 3 hours, until well chilled. When ready to serve, pour soup into serving bowls and garnish with chopped tomato, a dollop of sour cream and cilantro leaves.

SPICY GAZPACHO

This cold spicy tomato-based "liquid salad" makes the perfect lunch or first course for hot summer days or nights. It keeps well in the refrigerator for 3 to 4 days.

1 cup bread cubes, crust removed, preferably 1-2 days old
1/3 cup sherry vinegar
1 lb. fresh tomatoes
2 cups tomato juice
1/2 cup water
2 tbs. extra virgin olive oil
1 tbs. finely chopped fresh green or red chile
2 tomatillos, peeled, coarsely chopped, about 1/2 cup
1/3 cup coarsely chopped red onion
1/2 cup diced green bell pepper
1/2 cup diced red bell pepper
1 cup coarsely chopped peeled, seeded cucumber
1/2 tsp. ground cumin
salt and freshly ground pepper
1/2 cup chopped cilantro for garnish
Garlic Croutons for garnish, follows

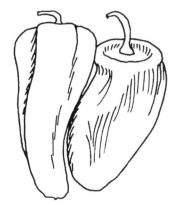

Place bread cubes in small bowl and cover with sherry vinegar. Let stand until bread softens. Peel tomatoes and squeeze out seeds and juice in a sieve over a bowl to catch juices. Cut tomatoes into chunks and place tomatoes and their juice in a blender or food processor container. Add softened bread cubes, 2 cups tomato juice, water, olive oil, chile, tomatillos, chopped onion, ¼ cup of the green bell pepper, ¼ cup of the red bell pepper, cucumber, cumin, salt and pepper. Process until well mixed but not smooth. Pour into a bowl or pitcher, cover and refrigerate for 2 to 3 hours before serving. To serve, ladle soup into bowls and sprinkle with remaining bell peppers and cilantro. Garnish with *Garlic Croutons*.

GARLIC GROUTONS
1 tbs. butter
1 tbs. olive oil
2 cloves garlic, peeled and smashed
4 slices bread, crusts removed, cut into ¾-inch cubes

Heat butter and oil in a medium skillet, add garlic and cook for 2 to 3 minutes until lightly brown. Discard garlic and sauté bread cubes in flavored oil until lightly browned and crisp.

SWEET POTATO SOUP

Servings: 4-6

This piquant creamy soup may be made ahead, refrigerated and reheated when ready to serve. It is a good choice for a fall or winter holiday menu.

2 tbs. butter
1 large onion, finely chopped
1 tbs. finely chopped fresh red or green chile
2 cloves garlic, finely chopped
1 tsp. *Chipotle Puree*, page 19
3-3½ cups chicken broth

2 lb. sweet potatoes, about 3, peeled, cut into ½-inch slices
2 tbs. lime juice
salt and freshly ground pepper
½ cup heavy cream
fresh cilantro leaves or sour cream and lime wedges for garnish

Melt butter in a large saucepan over medium heat, add onion and chile and sauté for 6 to 8 minutes, until onion is soft. Stir in garlic and cook for 1 to 2 minutes. Add *Chipotle Puree* and chicken broth; bring to a boil. Place sweet potato slices in broth with lime juice, salt and pepper. Cook over low heat, covered, for about 20 minutes, until potatoes are soft. Remove from heat, cool slightly and puree mixture with a food processor. Return soup to saucepan, add cream and reheat over low heat. Check seasoning. Serve in warmed soup bowls, garnished with fresh cilantro leaves, or with a dollop of sour cream and lime wedges.

GUACAMOLE

This classic dip is great with tortilla chips and sliced jicama, or spooned over a taco or tostada. The dark green bumpy-skinned Haas avocados have more flavor and a creamier texture than the smooth-skinned varieties.

2 ripe Haas avocados
2 tbs. finely diced red onion
1 tbs. minced fresh green or red chile
2 tbs. lime juice
salt and freshly ground pepper
¼ cup chopped cilantro leaves

Peel, seed and dice avocados into a bowl. Coarsely mash avocados with a fork. Add remaining ingredients and combine. Guacamole should have a lumpy texture and not be perfectly smooth. Cover with plastic wrap and refrigerate if not serving immediately.

VARIATION

Make a luncheon salad of lettuce greens and diced tomato. Top with a few cooked shrimp and a big spoonful of guacamole.

MUSHROOM AND BACON FRITTATA

*Serve this Italian-style frittata in wedges for breakfast or a picnic, or cut it into small squares for an appetizer. It can be served warm or at room temperature. Top with **Pico de Gallo**, page 148, or **Tomatillo Salsa**, page 151.*

2 slices bacon
5-6 green onions, white part only, thinly sliced
2-3 mushrooms, trimmed, thinly sliced
1 clove garlic, finely chopped
1 fresh hot red or green chile, finely chopped
5 eggs
salt and freshly ground pepper
1 tsp. Tabasco Jalapeño Sauce
2 tbs. finely chopped fresh parsley
2 tsp. olive oil
2-3 tbs. grated Parmesan cheese

Cut bacon into ½-inch pieces and sauté in a 7- or 8-inch ovenproof skillet until brown and crisp. Remove bacon and drain on paper towels. Pour out all but 2 tsp. bacon fat and sauté onions and mushrooms over medium heat for 3 to 4 minutes. Add garlic and chile and cook for 1 minute. Remove pan from heat. Preheat broiler.

In a small bowl, beat eggs, salt, pepper and Tabasco with a fork until well combined. Add bacon-mushroom mixture and parsley. Wipe out skillet, add olive oil and place over medium heat. Pour egg mixture into heated pan and cook until eggs start to set. Tilt pan and, with a fork, lift eggs around sides of pan so uncooked portion flows under cooked portion. When top is no longer liquid, sprinkle with Parmesan cheese and place under broiler 8 to 10 inches away from heat source for a few minutes, until top is lightly browned. Slide frittata out of pan onto a plate. Place serving plate upside down on top of frittata and flip over so top side is up. Blot any excess oil from surface with paper towels. Cut into wedges to serve.

VARIATION

Substitute ¼ cup each chopped green chile and roasted red pepper for the mushrooms. Add 1 to 2 tbs. toasted pine nuts.

MARINATED CHILE GOAT CHEESE

Makes 8 pieces

Marinate the goat cheese a day ahead and refrigerate. It will keep well for several days in the refrigerator. Use a round of cheese to top an individual salad, or use as an appetizer, or serve as a cheese course with toasts or crackers.

$1/2$ cup full-flavored olive oil
4 large cloves garlic, peeled, smashed
1 tsp. finely chopped fresh red or green
    chiles
1 log (11 oz.) semisoft goat cheese
$1/4$ tsp. red pepper flakes

$1/4$ tsp. dried thyme
$1/4$ tsp. crushed dried rosemary
generous grinds of black pepper
1 tbs. *Chile Pepper Vodka*, page 165,
    optional

Heat olive oil, garlic and fresh chiles in a small saucepan over low heat until garlic cloves are lightly browned. Do not burn. Remove from heat, strain, discard garlic and chiles and cool oil to room temperature. Cut cheese log into 8 equal rounds and arrange in a small pan or dish large enough to hold cheese slices in one layer. Sprinkle cheese with red pepper flakes, thyme, rosemary and black pepper. Drizzle with *Chile Pepper Vodka*, if using, and pour cooled oil over cheeses. Cover and refrigerate for 24 hours before using. Baste cheese with oil once or twice during marination. Serve at cool room temperature.

SPICY PECANS

The intriguing combination of hot and sweet flavors make these a great nibble or party fare.

2 cups raw unsalted pecan halves
2 tbs. vegetable oil
$\frac{1}{2}$ tsp. pure chile powder (see pages 11, 12)
$\frac{1}{2}$ tsp. kosher salt
$\frac{1}{4}$ tsp. onion powder
3 tbs. sugar

Preheat oven to 350°. Place pecans on a baking sheet and toast for 5 to 7 minutes. Do not allow to totally dry or start to brown. Heat vegetable oil in a large skillet over medium heat. Add toasted pecans, tossing to coat evenly with oil.

Combine chile powder, salt, onion powder and sugar in a small bowl and sprinkle mixture over pecans. Continue to cook and stir to coat pecans as sugar melts. When all sugar has melted and pecans are well coated, turn pecans out onto a baking sheet to cool. When cool, store in an airtight container.

HOT CHILE PEANUTS

Makes 2 cups

Easy and delicious, these spicy peanuts are a perfect accompaniment for beer. Use any leftover chile salt to dress hot buttered popcorn or use at the table for potatoes, eggs, corn on the cob and other vegetables.

CHILE SALT

2 tsp. kosher salt
2 tsp. ground cumin
1 tsp. pure New Mexico chile powder, medium-hot
½ tsp. ground coriander

½ tsp. hot dry mustard
½ tsp. onion powder
¼ tsp. garlic powder
1 tsp. sugar

1 large egg white
2 tsp. water

2 cups dry roasted, unsalted peanuts

Preheat oven to 225°. Combine chile salt ingredients with a spice mill or a mortar and pestle until a fine powder. Beat egg white and water in a small bowl with a fork until foamy. Pour through a strainer into a bowl and discard foam. Add peanuts to bowl and coat with egg mixture. Sprinkle 2 tbs. chile salt over peanuts, coating evenly. Spread peanuts on a rimmed baking sheet and bake for about 20 minutes, until egg white is set and peanuts are crunchy. Serve warm or store in an airtight container.

PINTO BEAN DIP

Makes 2 cups

This homemade bean dip is much better than the purchased variety. Use fresh vegetable pieces or tortilla chips for dipping, or spread in a quesadilla with sharp cheddar cheese and lots of chopped cilantro.

2 tsp. olive oil
1/2 cup finely chopped red onion
3 cloves garlic, finely chopped
1/2 tsp. ground cumin
1/2 tsp. pasilla chile powder
1 can (15 oz.) pinto beans, rinsed and
    drained
1 large tomato, peeled, seeded, chopped

1 1/2-2 tbs. finely chopped serrano or
    red Fresno chile
2 tbs. lime juice
2 tbs. yogurt or sour cream
2 tbs. chopped cilantro
salt and freshly ground pepper
cilantro leaves for garnish

In a small skillet over medium high heat, add oil and sauté onion to 4 to 5 minutes until soft. Add garlic, cumin and chile powder and cook for 2 to 3 minutes until spices release their fragrance. Place beans in a food processor workbowl and pulse 3 or 4 times to chop. Add tomato, chile, lime juice, yogurt, cilantro, salt, pepper and onion mixture to beans. Pulse to combine ingredients but do not process until totally smooth. Spoon into a serving bowl and garnish with cilantro, or refrigerate until ready to serve.

MAKING SMALL DISHES WITH CHILES   131

JAMAICAN PATTIES

Authentic patties are made with Scotch bonnet chiles. In this recipe, habanero chiles (equally searing hot) make a nicely spiced pattie. If you enjoy hot food, add more chiles or adjust cooked filling with Tabasco Sauce. The filling and pastry can be made a day ahead and baked just before serving. After they are baked, the patties can be reheated in a microwave or conventional oven.

CRUST

2 cups all-purpose flour
1/4 tsp. baking powder
1/2 tsp. salt

1 egg yolk
1/2 cup vegetable shortening
about 1/3 cup ice water

Add flour, baking powder and salt to a food processor workbowl. Pulse once or twice to combine. Add egg yolk and shortening; pulse until mixture resembles coarse meal. With processor running, slowly add ice water until mixture comes together and forms a ball. Remove dough from bowl, wrap in plastic wrap and refrigerate for 30 minutes or longer before rolling out.

FILLING

1 cup fresh white breadcrumbs, crust removed
1/3 cup milk
1 tbs. vegetable oil
1 habanero chile, stemmed, seeded, finely minced

1/2 cup finely chopped onion
2 tsp. curry powder
1/2 tsp. dried thyme
1/2 lb. lean ground beef
salt and freshly ground pepper

1 egg yolk beaten with 1 tsp. water for glaze

In a small bowl, soak breadcrumbs in milk for 10 minutes until liquid is absorbed. Add oil to a nonstick skillet over medium heat. Sauté chile and onion for 2 to 3 minutes; add curry powder and thyme. Stir until curry releases its fragrance. Crumble ground beef into skillet and cook until no longer pink, but do not brown. Add breadcrumb mixture, salt and pepper. Mix well, reduce heat and simmer until most of the moisture has evaporated. Cool.

Preheat oven to 375°. Roll out pastry to a thickness of about 1/8 inch. Using a small saucer as a guide, cut rounds about 5 to 6 inches in diameter. Place 1/4 cup of the filling on half of the dough. Fold over the other half and seal edges by crimping with a fork. Prick surface with a fork to allow steam to escape. Brush with egg yolk mixture. Bake for 20 to 25 minutes, or until golden brown. Eat hot or at room temperature.

SEVICHE

This Mexican seafood salad makes a delicious hot-weather lunch or appetizer. The citrus juice "cooks" the scallops and gives them a firm texture. Do not marinate any longer than 4 to 5 hours because the texture changes and the scallops turn mushy. Serve on lettuce leaves as a salad or with tortilla chips as an appetizer.

1 lb. small bay scallops
1/4 cup fresh lime juice
1/4 cup fresh lemon juice
1/3 cup fresh orange juice
2 tbs. finely minced fresh red or green chile
3-4 green onions, white part only, finely chopped

1/2 tsp. crushed dried oregano
2 medium tomatoes, peeled, seeded, chopped
1 avocado, peeled, seeded, chopped
1 tbs. olive oil
salt and freshly ground pepper
cilantro leaves for garnish
lettuce leaves or tortilla chips

Place scallops in a small glass or stainless bowl or in a heavy locking plastic bag and pour in citrus juices. Cover and refrigerate for about 3 to 4 hours; stir once or twice. Scallops will be firm and turn from translucent to opaque when marinated. Drain scallops and place in a serving bowl. Add remaining ingredients, mix well, garnish with cilantro leaves and serve lightly chilled on lettuce leaves, or with tortilla chips.

SPICY MUSTARD SHRIMP

This appetizer is ready in just a few minutes. Serve with toothpicks and lots of napkins, or arrange shrimp and avocado slices over salad greens for a first course.

1 lb. medium shrimp, peeled, deveined
1 tsp. salt

MARINADE

2 tsp. finely chopped shallot
2 small green jalapeño chiles, stemmed, seeded, finely chopped
2 small red jalapeño chiles, stemmed, seeded, finely chopped

2 tbs. Dijon mustard
2 tbs. rice vinegar
3 tbs. olive oil
2 tbs. finely chopped cilantro
freshly ground pepper

cilantro leaves for garnish

Bring 3 or 4 quarts of water to boil in a large pot, add salt and cook shrimp for 1 to 2 minutes. Do not overcook. Shrimp will turn pink and should be slightly firm to the touch. Drain immediately and rinse with cold water to stop cooking process.

Combine marinade ingredients in a small bowl. Pat shrimp dry with a paper towel, place in a serving bowl and pour marinade over shrimp. Toss to coat shrimp with marinade. Cover bowl with plastic wrap and refrigerate for 20 to 30 minutes. Garnish with cilantro leaves before serving.

QUESADILLAS

Quesadillas can be served anytime. They make delicious, easy appetizers, or an entrée for one for breakfast or lunch. Traditionally the tortillas are heated in a nonstick skillet just long enough to melt the cheese and warm the filling. Brushing the outside of the tortilla with melted butter or vegetable oil produces a flakier crust. To make several at a time, bake them in a hot oven for 8 to 10 minutes. They brown nicely even without brushing with fat.

CRAB QUESADILLA

Servings: 2-3 as appetizer, 1 as entrée

2 flour tortillas, 8-inch
1/3 cup flaked crabmeat
1/2 tsp. Dijon mustard
salt and freshly ground pepper

1/3 cup grated pepper Jack cheese
2 tbs. diced roasted poblano chile
6-8 cherry tomatoes, cut in half
2-3 tbs. cilantro leaves

Preheat oven to 450°. Line a baking sheet with foil. Lay a tortilla on foil. Mix crabmeat with mustard, salt and pepper. Sprinkle tortilla with cheese and evenly arrange pieces of crab, chile, tomatoes and cilantro over cheese. Top with remaining tortilla and lightly press tortillas together. Bake for 8 to 10 minutes, or until lightly browned. Cut into wedges and serve immediately.

RED ONION QUESADILLA

Servings: 2-3 as appetizer, 1 as entrée

Caramelized onions, olives and a little tahini give this quesadilla Mediterranean flavor. Middle Eastern markets stock the tahini (sesame paste) in jars and it keeps for several weeks refrigerated. If you don't have tahini, substitute smooth peanut butter. Garnish with cumin-flavored yogurt and chopped mint.

1-2 tsp. *Hot Chile Oil*, page 162, or
    purchased chile oil
1 medium red onion, thinly sliced
1 tbs. water
1 clove garlic, finely chopped
3 flour tortillas, 8-inch
1-2 tbs. tahini

10-12 fresh basil leaves, cut into thin
    ribbons
1/2 cup grated Monterey Jack cheese
1 tbs. grated Parmesan cheese
6-8 kalamata or niçoise olives, pitted,
    chopped

Preheat oven to 450°. Heat chile oil in a small skillet, add onion and sauté for 3 to 4 minutes. Add water to skillet, cover and continue to cook for 8 to 10 minutes, until onion is very soft and starting to brown. Add garlic to onion slices and cook for 1 minute. On a baking sheet covered with foil, place 1 tortilla. Spread with tahini and sprinkle with basil. Top with second tortilla. Spread tortilla with onions, cheeses and olives. Cover with third tortilla. Bake for 8 to 10 minutes until cheese is hot and quesadilla is lightly browned. Cut into wedges and serve immediately.

ROASTED VEGETABLE QUESADILLAS

Servings: 4-6 as appetizer, 2 as entrée

Roast your favorite vegetables for a delicious filling for 2 quesadillas.

1 small Japanese eggplant
½ red bell pepper
1 small poblano chile
2 onion slices, about ¼-inch thick
1 tbs. full-flavored olive oil
4 flour tortillas, 8-inch

4 roasted garlic cloves, page 19, mashed
1 cup coarsely grated mozzarella or
   Monterey Jack cheese
2 tbs. grated Parmesan cheese
salt and freshly ground pepper
¼ tsp. red pepper flakes

Preheat broiler and line a rimmed baking sheet with foil. Remove stem from eggplant, cut into ¼-inch slices lengthwise and place on baking sheet with bell pepper, chile and onion slices. Brush eggplant and onion slices with olive oil. Broil until eggplant is lightly browned, 3 to 4 minutes each side, and bell pepper and chile are charred. Remove from oven, put into a covered bowl and steam for 10 minutes before peeling. Preheat oven to 450°. Replace foil on baking sheet. Place 2 tortillas on baking sheet, spread each with garlic and distribute cheese and vegetables. Season with salt, pepper and red pepper flakes. Top each with another tortilla. Bake at 450° for 8 to 10 minutes until lightly browned. Cut into wedges and serve immediately.

SHRIMP TACOS

*These tacos are made with small fresh corn tortillas, but you could use preformed crisp taco shells and add extra shredded lettuce and avocado pieces. To vary, spread warm tortillas with **Cilantro Pesto**, page 156, before filling.*

½ lb. uncooked medium shrimp, peeled, deveined
1 avocado, peeled, seeded, cut into ½-inch cubes
1 medium-sized ripe tomato, peeled, seeded, chopped
2 small green onions, white part only, finely chopped

1 tbs. finely chopped fresh red or green chile
1 tbs. lime juice
2 tbs. coarsely chopped cilantro leaves
salt and freshly ground pepper
8 corn tortillas, 6-inch
8 leafy lettuce leaves

Cook shrimp in boiling salted water for 2 to 3 minutes, just until they turn pink and are slightly firm to the touch. Rinse with cold water to stop cooking. Drain well and place in a bowl. Add avocado, tomato, onions, chile, lime juice, cilantro, salt and pepper. Heat corn tortillas in a microwave for 25 to 30 seconds, or one at a time in an ungreased skillet over medium heat for 10 to 15 seconds. Place a lettuce leaf on each tortilla, top with avocado shrimp filling, fold up sides and eat out of hand.

SPICY CHICKEN WINGS

Makes 20 pieces

Chicken wings make great appetizers, snacks or lunch box fare. Do them ahead and reheat in the microwave, or serve hot from the oven. Sambal oelek, hoisin sauce and Shao Xing rice wine are found in the supermarket's Asian food section.

10 chicken wings
2 tbs. soy sauce
2 tbs. Shao Xing rice wine or dry sherry
2 tsp. sambal oelek (see page 10)
3 tbs. hoisin sauce

1 tbs. vegetable oil
2 green onions, white part only, finely chopped
1 tbs. finely chopped ginger root

Cut off wing tips and cut each wing into 2 pieces at the joint. Trim off excess skin. Save wing tips and other trimmings to make chicken stock. Combine remaining ingredients in a small bowl. Place chicken wings in a locking plastic bag, add marinade, close bag and marinate in the refrigerator for 8 hours or overnight.

Preheat oven to 375°. Line a rimmed baking sheet with foil. Place a rack over foil and spray with nonstick cooking spray. Remove wings from marinade and place on rack. Bake for 25 minutes, turn over and continue to bake for 25 minutes until wings are fully cooked and nicely browned.

SALSAS, SAUCES AND SPECIALTIES

Salsa comes from Mexican cuisine and can be either fresh or cooked. The simplest are made of fresh tomato or fruit paired with some type of onion, hot chiles, acid in the form of lime or lemon juice, or vinegar, and fresh or dried herbs. To make your own fresh salsa, use the freshest ingredients and eat it the same day. It is suggested that salt be added just before serving fresh salsas, particularly those containing tomatoes, because the salt causes the tomato liquid to be released and the mixture gets watery. Homemade cooked salsas keep in the refrigerator for a few days. Use commercial salsas within a month or two after opening. Salsas are great to have on hand to spice up quesadillas and dips, or to spoon over grilled fish or chicken.

Cilantro is a favorite herb for salsa. It also makes great pesto. Add *Cilantro Pesto* to mayonnaise for salads or a sandwich spread, slather it on tortillas when you make quesadillas, and spoon it over grilled fish or chicken.

Our chile pantry includes *Hot Chile Oil*, wonderful brushed on little new potatoes just before grilling, for pizza crusts, for popping popcorn and many other uses. It is easy to make and keeps well.

Dried chiles are available year-round, in both whole and powdered form. Make *Dried Chile Paste* from an assortment, or just one or two kinds of dried chiles when you have time. Keep it on hand and add a spoonful or two to soups, stews and meat dishes. Combine it with fresh or canned tomatoes for a winter salsa.

With fresh habanero chiles, make Jamaican *Jerk Rub for Pork or Chicken.* If you enjoy really hot food, the habanero is worth trying for its hot fruity flavor.

Chile Tartar Sauce is made with pickled jalapeño nacho slices. Add more jalapeños if these aren't hot enough.

BLOOD ORANGE SALSA

Blood oranges are becoming more available now that they are being grown in the United States. With their rich dark color and firm acidity they make a striking and piquant salsa.

3 blood oranges, about 1 lb.
1 tbs. finely chopped red onion
1 tbs. finely chopped fresh red or green chile
1 tbs. red wine vinegar
1 tbs. olive oil
salt and freshly ground pepper
½ cup finely chopped cilantro leaves

With a sharp knife, cut down sides of orange and remove peel and white pith. Over a bowl, cut down both sides of membrane to release segments. Squeeze any juice remaining in membrane into bowl. Cut segments into ½-inch chunks. Add remaining ingredients and toss. Cover and refrigerate until ready to serve.

MANGO CUCUMBER SALSA

Tangy mango and cool cucumber pieces make a great salsa to serve with grilled fish or chicken. This can be made a day ahead and refrigerated. Add salt and pepper just before serving. The mango has a very large seed that clings tenaciously to the fruit, which must be cut away from the seed with a sharp knife.

1 medium mango
½ cup diced cucumber
1-2 tbs. diced red onion
1 tsp. finely minced serrano chiles
½ tsp. ground cumin
2 tbs. lime juice
1 tsp. olive oil
salt and freshly ground pepper

Peel mango and cut fruit from large seed. Squeeze juice from pulp surrounding seed into a bowl; discard seed. Cut mango into ½-inch pieces and add to bowl with remaining ingredients, except salt and pepper; mix well. Set aside for 20 minutes for flavors to develop. Season with salt and pepper just before serving.

FRESH PAPAYA AND AVOCADO SALSA

Makes 1¾ cups

This easy salsa is great with quesadillas, grilled pork, chicken or seafood. Add salt just before serving. When it is added early, the fruits release too much liquid.

1 medium papaya, peeled, seeded, diced into ½-inch pieces
1 medium avocado, peeled, seeded, diced into ½-inch pieces
2 tbs. lime juice
½ tsp. peeled, grated ginger root
2 green onions, white part only, thinly sliced
2 tsp. finely chopped red serrano or other fresh hot chile
2 tsp. olive oil
6-8 fresh basil leaves, cut into ribbons
2 tbs. finely chopped cilantro leaves
salt and freshly ground pepper

In a small bowl, combine ingredients, except salt and pepper, mix well. Set aside for 20 or 30 minutes for flavors to combine. Season with salt and pepper just before serving.

VARIATION

Fold in ½ cup cooked small salad shrimp or diced cooked chicken and serve over salad greens as a luncheon salad for 2.

PICO DE GALLO

Make this classic fresh tomato salsa just before serving, because the tomatoes rapidly release juice after salt is added. Serve as a dip with **Chile Lovers' Tortilla Chips***, page 119, or spoon over* **Mushroom and Bacon Frittata***, page 126. Double this recipe if you are serving a crowd.*

2 medium tomatoes, cored, seeded, chopped
1 fresh red or green chile, stemmed, seeded, finely chopped
1-2 tbs. finely chopped red onion
1 small clove garlic, finely chopped
2 tbs. lime juice
2-3 tbs. chopped fresh cilantro leaves
salt and freshly ground pepper

Combine ingredients, except salt and pepper, in a serving bowl. Add salt and pepper just before serving.

PINEAPPLE, CUCUMBER AND JICAMA SALSA

Serve this fresh minty salsa with grilled fish, chicken or lamb.

1 cup diced fresh pineapple
1/2 cup peeled, seeded, diced cucumber
1/2 cup peeled, diced jicama
2 tbs. minced red onion
2 tbs. minced serrano or red Fresno chile
1 tsp. brown sugar
1 tsp. ground cumin
1 tbs. olive oil
2 tbs. lime juice
1 tbs. chopped cilantro leaves
8-10 fresh mint leaves, cut into ribbons
salt and freshly ground pepper

Place ingredients, except salt and pepper, in a bowl and toss to mix well. Set aside for 20 minutes before serving so flavors can combine. Add salt and pepper just before serving.

ROASTED TOMATO AND CHILE SALSA

Makes 1½ cups

Roasting the tomatoes and garlic gives the salsa a rich, light smoky flavor. Serve with grilled sausages or hamburgers, or spoon over scrambled eggs. This salsa can be made ahead and will keep in the refrigerator for 3 to 4 days.

2 dried ancho or New Mexico chiles
6 plum tomatoes
6 cloves garlic, unpeeled
1 medium red onion, peeled, cut into
   ½-inch-thick slices

½ tsp. dried oregano
¼ cup lime juice
1 tbs. minced jalapeño or serrano chile
¼ cup chopped cilantro
salt and freshly ground pepper

Remove stems and seeds from dried chiles. In a nonstick skillet over medium heat, toast dried chile pieces for 1 to 2 minutes, or until chiles become pliable. Do not burn. Remove skillet from heat. Cover chiles with boiling water and soak for 15 to 20 minutes, or until soft. Drain and place in a blender container.

Preheat broiler. While chiles are soaking, line a shallow pan with foil and place tomatoes, garlic and onion slices on foil. Broil for 10 to 15 minutes, turning vegetables until lightly charred on all sides. Remove from oven. When cool enough to handle, cut out tomato cores but leave blackened peel on tomatoes. Peel garlic, coarsely chop onion slices and place vegetables in a blender container with remaining ingredients. Process until almost smooth. Check seasoning and refrigerate until serving.

TOMATILLO SALSA

Makes 1½ cups

*Spoon this all-purpose salsa over grilled chicken or fish or **Crab Enchiladas**, page 38. Use it to garnish quesadillas, or serve with tortilla chips. This salsa will keep in the refrigerator for 3 to 4 days. Serve it at room temperature.*

1 lb. fresh tomatillos
4 serrano chiles, stemmed
⅓ cup chopped onion
2 tbs. chopped cilantro leaves
2 tbs. chopped Italian parsley
2 tbs. vegetable oil
salt and freshly ground pepper

Remove tomatillo husks and rinse with cold water. Place tomatillos and chiles in a saucepan, cover with water and bring to a boil. Lower heat and simmer uncovered for about 10 minutes, or until tomatillos are barely soft. Reserve ¼ cup of the cooking liquid and drain tomatillos and chiles. Pour tomatillos, chiles and reserved cooking liquid into a blender container. Add onion, cilantro and parsley and process until smooth. Heat vegetable oil in a large skillet and add tomatillo mixture. Season with salt and pepper. Simmer over medium heat for 8 to 10 minutes until sauce thickens, stirring frequently. Allow sauce to cool before serving.

WATERMELON AND PINEAPPLE SALSA

Makes 2 cups

The flavor of summer is in this cooling fruit salsa. Serve with grilled fish or chicken, or with quesadillas. Make this salsa just before serving.

1 cup diced watermelon, rind and seeds removed
1 cup diced fresh pineapple
2 tbs. thinly sliced green onion, white part only
1 tbs. minced jalapeño or red Fresno chile
1 tsp. ground cumin
1 tbs. olive oil
2 tbs. lime juice
2 tbs. chopped cilantro
8-10 fresh basil leaves, cut into thin ribbons
salt and freshly ground pepper

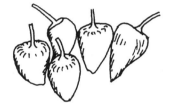

Place ingredients in a bowl and toss lightly to combine.

FRESH CORN RELISH

Serve this flavorful relish with sandwiches or hamburgers, or to accompany grilled fish or chicken. This is better if made a day ahead and refrigerated to allow flavors to blend.

¼ cup cider vinegar
2 tbs. lemon juice
¼ cup brown sugar, packed
1 tbs. finely chopped fresh red or green chile
½ tsp. mustard seeds, or ¼ tsp. hot dry mustard

½ tsp. celery seeds
pinch turmeric
2 cups fresh corn kernels, about 5-6 ears
½ cup diced red bell pepper
salt and freshly ground pepper
chopped cilantro leaves for garnish

Combine vinegar, lemon juice, sugar, chile, mustard and celery seeds, and tumeric in a medium saucepan. Bring mixture to a boil, lower heat and simmer for 2 to 3 minutes. Add fresh corn and red pepper pieces, cover and cook for 5 minutes. Remove from heat and pour into a glass or stainless steel bowl; season with salt and pepper. Cover and refrigerate overnight. Remove from refrigerator 30 minutes before serving. Taste for seasoning and garnish with chopped cilantro leaves before serving.

MANGO AND RED PEPPER CHUTNEY

Makes 2 cups

Serve some of this flavorful chutney with curry or as an accompaniment for grilled fish. It is a nice accent for pork or turkey sandwiches, too. Use firm, not quite ripe, fruit for this chutney. This keeps well in the refrigerator.

1 tbs. vegetable oil
1 cup diced onion
½ cup diced red bell pepper
1 large clove garlic, minced
1 tsp. finely chopped, peeled ginger root
1½ tsp. minced red or green serrano chile
1¾-2 cups chopped peeled mango, about 2 large
⅓ cup brown sugar, packed
½ tsp. ground ginger
½ tsp. allspice
½ cup cider vinegar
½ cup water
½ tsp. salt

Heat oil in a large nonstick skillet over medium heat and sauté onion for 4 to 5 minutes to soften. Add red pepper, garlic, ginger and chiles and cook for 2 to 3 minutes. Add remaining ingredients, bring to a boil and simmer uncovered for 25 to 30 minutes. Stir occasionally. Mixture will thicken as liquid evaporates. Watch carefully for the last 10 minutes of cooking, and stir frequently to keep chutney from sticking to bottom of pan. Remove from heat and cool before serving.

CILANTRO PESTO

*Include a little of this pungent pesto in quesadillas or drizzle over grilled sausages or fish. Use it as a filling for little cherry tomatoes, or make **Cilantro Pesto Mayonnaise**, page 157.*

3 cloves garlic
2 cups cilantro leaves, including tender
    stems, packed
1 tbs. minced fresh red or green chile
2 tsp. lime juice

1 tsp. dried oregano
½ cup toasted pine nuts
⅓ cup olive oil
salt and freshly ground pepper

In a food processor workbowl, with motor running, drop garlic cloves through the feed tube. Scrape down sides and add cilantro and chile. Process until finely chopped. Add remaining ingredients and process to a smooth paste. Cover tightly and refrigerate until ready to use.

VARIATION

Toss some hot cooked pasta with *Cilantro Pesto*, grated fresh Parmesan cheese and a peeled, seeded, diced fresh tomato.

CILANTRO PESTO MAYONNAISE

Use this piquant spread on chicken or pork sandwiches or as a dressing for a shrimp or scallop salad. It also makes great deviled eggs. This dressing will keep for 3 to 4 days in the refrigerator. Double the recipe if you like.

½ cup mayonnaise
2 tbs. *Cilantro Pesto*, page 156
1-2 tbs. milk

Combine mayonnaise and pesto in a small bowl, whisking until smooth. Add a little milk to thin mayonnaise to desired consistency. Refrigerate until ready to serve.

CHILE TARTAR SAUCE

Makes about 1 cup

This is a quick jalapeño-spiked tartar sauce to serve with grilled fish or cooked shrimp, or use it with salmon or crab cakes. Make it 1 to 2 hours ahead and refrigerate so flavors have time to blend. This recipe doubles easily and will keep for several days in the refrigerator.

½ cup mayonnaise
2 tbs. finely chopped pickled jalapeño nacho slices
2 green onions, white part only, finely chopped
½ tsp. Dijon mustard
½ tsp. dried oregano
2 tbs. finely chopped fresh parsley
¼ tsp. Tabasco Jalapeño Sauce
freshly ground pepper

Place mayonnaise in a small bowl, add remaining ingredients and stir until well combined. Refrigerate until ready to serve.

CRANBERRY CHILE RELISH

Makes 2½ cups

Serve this spicy fresh cranberry relish with the holiday ham or turkey, or to accent chicken or cheese quesadillas. This keeps well in the refrigerator for 3 to 4 days. It's better made a few hours ahead and refrigerated so flavors have a chance to blend.

1 large orange
⅓ cup sugar
½ tsp. New Mexico or pasilla chile powder
2 cups cranberries
1 tbs. finely minced fresh red or green chile
½ cup toasted walnuts
½ tsp. salt

Cut orange peel, including pith, from orange, coarsely chop and place in a food processor workbowl with sugar. Remove seeds, coarsely chop orange pulp and reserve. Process orange peel and sugar mixture until finely chopped. Add chile powder, cranberries, fresh chile, walnuts and salt to workbowl and pulse until well chopped. Add reserved orange pulp and pulse 4 to 5 times to blend into mixture. Pour into a bowl, cover and refrigerate until ready to serve.

HABANERO JELLY

Spoon this attractive, spicy, orange-hued jelly over a block of cream cheese and serve it with crackers for an impromptu appetizer. Use it to baste roasted chicken or pork. The fruitiness of the hot habanero chile adds a more interesting flavor than the one-dimensional heat provided by jalapeños. Use great care when handling this hot chile, and measure ingredients exactly.

1 large red bell pepper, stemmed, seeded
1 medium-sized tart unpeeled green apple, cored, coarsely chopped
1/2-1 habanero chile, stemmed, seeded, chopped
2 cups apple juice, plus more if needed
1/4 cup cider vinegar
1/2 tsp. kosher salt
4 cups sugar
1/2 tsp. butter or margarine
1 pkg. (11.7 oz.) Sure-Jell

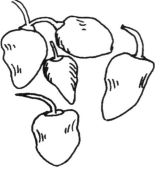

Chop bell pepper and apple with a food processor and combine with chile, apple juice, vinegar and salt in a medium nonaluminum saucepan. Bring to a boil, lower heat and simmer for 20 minutes. Strain hot mixture through several layers of cheesecloth into a 4-cup measuring cup. If necessary, add enough juice to bring liquid up to 2½ cups. Wash saucepan. Return mixture to saucepan and bring to a full boil. Add butter and Sure-Jell and bring jelly back to a full boil, stirring constantly. Add sugar all at once and return mixture to a rolling boil. Boil for exactly 1 minute. Remove from heat, skim off foam, pour into sterlized jars and seal, or refrigerate for as long as 3 months.

HOT CHILE OIL

Makes 1 cup

The small bottles of hot chile pepper oil available in Asian and specialty groceries are quite expensive and full of red food coloring. When you make your own, you are sure of the ingredients and can control the heat.

1 cup canola, peanut or corn oil
6 small or 4 large chiles de arbol, or 2 tbs. red pepper flakes

Remove stems from chiles and shake out seeds. In a small saucepan over low heat, cook vegetable oil and chiles for several minutes until chiles turn dark brown; do not allow them to burn. Remove from heat and cool. Strain cooled oil into a small bottle or jar, and store tightly capped in a cool place. This will keep for several months.

USES FOR HOT CHILE OIL

- Brush on pizza crust before adding sauce, cheese and other toppings.
- Use in popcorn popper, or drizzle a small amount over microwaved or air-popped popcorn.
- Use 1-2 tsp. in any stir-fried seafood or vegetable dish.
- Add to any tomato-based pasta sauce.
- Use a teaspoon with the butter to make an omelet or fried eggs.

DRIED CHILE PASTE

Makes 1½ cups

This piquant, flavorful condiment keeps well in the refrigerator, and a spoonful or two adds a little zip to stews, bean dishes or glazes for roasted meats. For a quick dipping salsa, combine equal amounts of chile paste with fresh or canned tomato pieces, and top with chopped cilantro.

3 oz. assorted dried chiles (pasilla, ancho, guajillo, arbol, New Mexico, cascabel, etc.)
2 tbs. cider vinegar

1 tsp. ground cumin
1 tsp. dried oregano
½ tsp. salt
⅓ cup water, or more

Wipe chiles clean with a moistened paper towel. Briefly rinse crinkled, bent chiles under running water. Break chiles open and discard seeds and stems. In a heavy skillet over medium heat, toast chiles briefly until they soften and are lightly browned. Do not burn. Place toasted chiles in a bowl, cover with boiling water and soak for 20 minutes. Lift chiles from soaking liquid with tongs or a slotted spoon, leaving sand and debris in bottom of bowl. Coarsely chop chiles and place in a blender container with remaining ingredients. Blend on high until mixture is smooth, scraping down sides of blender once or twice. Add a little more water if needed to make a thick but pourable liquid. Taste and add a little more cumin or oregano if desired.

JERK RUB FOR PORK OR CHICKEN

Coats 2 pork tenderloins
or 10 chicken thighs

Use this spicy Jamaican-style marinade for pork or chicken. Be sure to wear plastic or rubber gloves when handling the habanero chile and when rubbing the paste into the meat. The meat should marinate for at least 4 hours or overnight.

2 tbs. lime juice
1 tbs. vegetable oil
8 green onions, white part only,
    coarsely chopped
1 habanero chile, stemmed, seeded,
    coarsely chopped
2 tbs. allspice

1/4 tsp. ground nutmeg
1/2 tsp. freshly ground pepper
1/4 tsp. ground cinnamon
1/2 tsp. salt
2 pork tenderloins or 10 chicken thighs,
    skinned

Place lime juice and oil in a blender or food processor container, add onions and chile and blend to a smooth paste. Add remaining spices and pulse a few times to blend.

Wearing gloves, massage jerk mixture into pork or chicken and marinate in the refrigerator for at least 4 hours or overnight. Cook on a hot grill, or roast pork at 375° for 30 to 35 minutes or until it reaches 165°. Chicken should be placed on a rack and roasted for 45 to 50 minutes, or to a temperature of 185°.

CHILE PEPPER VODKA

Makes 25 oz. (1 fifth)

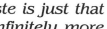

Imported European pepper vodka is quite expensive and the taste is just that of hot dried red chiles. Making your own is easy and yields an infinitely more flavorful drink. The habanero chile gives vodka an elusive citrus-apricot flavor, and all the heat you want. Start with this recipe. You can always add another chile if it is not hot enough. Try this with tequilla, too.

1 bottle (25 oz.) inexpensive vodka or tequilla (1 fifth)
1 habanero chile

Wear rubber gloves or use a knife and fork to handle the chile. Cut off stem and cut chile into quarters. Place chile pieces in vodka and recap bottle. Place in a cool place and allow chiles to macerate for 24 hours (no longer). Taste carefully and decide if your heat tolerance level has been reached. Macerate longer, or add another chile if desired. When hot enough, remove chile pieces and store bottle in the freezer.

VARIATION

Whole dried red arbol chiles can also be used to make pepper vodka very similar to the imported ones. Wash chiles, leave stems on, and use 3 to 4 in a fifth of vodka. Taste after 24 hours and adjust as directed.

PERFECT BLOODY MARY

Servings: 1

Our idea of a great Bloody Mary is one that has a nice bite and dominant tomato flavor. This recipe uses the powdered Japanese horseradish, wasabi, and some **Chile Pepper Vodka**, *page 165, for a spicy note. If you don't have pepper vodka, substitute ½ tsp. or more of Tabasco Jalapeño Sauce. If the tomato juice is cold and the vodka is kept in the freezer, there won't be as much dilution from melting ice.*

6 oz. tomato juice
½ tsp. Worcestershire sauce
generous amount freshly ground pepper
dash celery salt
¼ tsp. wasabi powder
1 oz. *Chile Pepper Vodka*, or regular vodka
generous squeeze fresh lime or lemon juice
1 stalk celery for garnish

Stir all ingredients together, except celery stalk, and pour over ice cubes. Stir and serve with a tender celery stalk.

INDEX

SERVE CREATIVE, EASY, NUTRITIOUS MEALS WITH nitty gritty® COOKBOOKS

Edible Pockets for Every Meal
Cooking With Chile Peppers
Oven and Rotisserie Roasting
Risottos, Paellas and Other Rice
  Specialties
Entrées From Your Bread Machine
Muffins, Nut Breads and More
Healthy Snacks for Kids
100 Dynamite Desserts
Recipes for Yogurt Cheese
Sautés
Cooking in Porcelain
Appetizers
Casseroles
The Best Bagels are made at home*
  (*perfect for your bread machine)
The Toaster Oven Cookbook
Skewer Cooking on the Grill
Creative Mexican Cooking
Extra-Special Crockery Pot Recipes
Slow Cooking
Cooking in Clay
Marinades
Deep Fried Indulgences

Cooking with Parchment Paper
The Garlic Cookbook
From Your Ice Cream Maker
Cappuccino/Espresso: The Book of
  Beverages
The Best Pizza is made at home*
  (*perfect for your bread machine)
The Well Dressed Potato
Convection Oven Cookery
The Steamer Cookbook
The Pasta Machine Cookbook
The Versatile Rice Cooker
The Dehydrator Cookbook
The Bread Machine Cookbook
The Bread Machine Cookbook II
The Bread Machine Cookbook III
The Bread Machine Cookbook IV:
  Whole Grains and Natural Sugars
The Bread Machine Cookbook V:
  Favorite Recipes from 100 Kitchens
The Bread Machine Cookbook VI:
  *Hand-Shaped Breads from the
  Dough Cycle*

Worldwide Sourdoughs From Your
  Bread Machine
Recipes for the Pressure Cooker
The New Blender Book
The Sandwich Maker Cookbook
Waffles
Indoor Grilling
The Coffee Book
The Juicer Books I and II
Bread Baking (traditional)
No Salt, No Sugar, No Fat Cookbook
Cooking for 1 or 2
Quick and Easy Pasta Recipes
The 9x13 Pan Cookbook
Recipes for the Loaf Pan
Low Fat American Favorites
Now That's Italian!
Healthy Cooking on the Run
The Wok
Favorite Seafood Recipes
New International Fondue Cookbook
Favorite Cookie Recipes
Flatbreads From Around the World

For a free catalog, write or call:
Bristol Publishing Enterprises, Inc.
P.O. Box 1737, San Leandro, CA 94577
(800) 346-4889; in California, (510) 895-4461